LT.-COL. SIR W. A. WAYLAND, J.P.

A
SHORT HISTORY
OF THE
39th (DEPTFORD)
Divisional Artillery
1915–1918

by

Lt.-Col. H. W. WIEBKIN, M.C.

(Late R.F.A.)

The Naval & Military Press Ltd

published in association with

FIREPOWER
The Royal Artillery Museum
Woolwich

Published by
The Naval & Military Press Ltd
Unit 10 Ridgewood Industrial Park,
Uckfield, East Sussex,
TN22 5QE England
Tel: +44 (0) 1825 749494
Fax: +44 (0) 1825 765701
www.naval-military-press.com

in association with

FIREPOWER
The Royal Artillery Museum, Woolwich
www.firepower.org.uk

PREFACE

N the formation of the 39th (Deptford) Divisional Artillery, and again just preparatory to proceeding to France, Sir W. A. Wayland, then Mayor of Deptford, requested, on behalf of the Borough Council, that if possible a record of the service of the Deptford Division might be kept, so that after the war such record could be placed amongst the archives in the Town Hall, Deptford.

Many locally raised units and formations were recruited throughout the British Empire similar to the formation of the Deptford Artillery, and possibly some can show a better war record than that briefly described in this book, but Deptford can well be proud of its achievement in producing a sufficient number of volunteers to form a complete Divisional Artillery in addition to a Heavy Artillery Battery and large numbers of recruits for local Territorial regiments.

In compiling this brief account of the services of the 39th Divisional Artillery, it has been borne in mind that, for the book to be within the reach of the men who served in the Division, the cost of production and printing must be kept to a minimum.

References to maps and the reproduction of maps have been purposely omitted with this object in view, as also the specific acts of gallantry for which the many honours and awards were made.

Therefore, in fulfilment of the request of Lt.-Col. Sir William Wayland, J.P., this brief account of the services of the 39th (Deptford) Divisional Artillery is written.

11, UPPER GROVE,
   SOUTH NORWOOD,
      LONDON, S.E.25.

September, 1923.

CONTENTS

		PAGE.
FOREWORD	.. ..	1
TRAINING PERIOD	.. ..	6
OFF TO FRANCE	.. ..	10
IN THE LINE	.. ..	11
THE SOMME	.. ..	14
YPRES	.. ..	19
THE GREAT RETREAT	.. ..	25
THE ADVANCE	.. ..	30

卐 卐 卐

APPENDICES

"A"	.. ..	TABLE OF UNITS
"B"	.. .. ..	NOMINAL ROLLS OF OFFICERS
"C"	.. ..	CASUALTIES TO OFFICERS
"D"	.. ..	CASUALTIES TO MEN
"E"	.. ..	HONOURS AND AWARDS

卐 卐 卐

Frontispiece :
Lt.-Col. SIR WILLIAM A. WAYLAND, J.P.,
former Mayor of Deptford.

FOREWORD

HE Hour and the Man ! Historians find a fascination in pointing to cases in which, with the striking of the Hour, the Man has stepped forth, prepared to bear upon his broad shoulders the burden of responsibility which events are shaping. This story of the 39th Divisional Artillery concerns the Hour, the Man—and then the Other Men ! To Deptford belongs the honour of giving birth to the 39th Divisional Artillery. The attendant circumstances are sufficiently interesting—almost unique—to justify their relation in detail.

First, the Hour ! It was the month of May, 1915. The War Office was clamouring for men : ordinary methods of recruiting were proving inadequate to supply our nation's need, and conscription had not yet been adopted.

The situation on the battle-fronts at the moment was such as to try our fortitude. In April hopes had been entertained that something more than a dent would be made in the opposing line, and that both we and the French would have noteworthy successes to chronicle. This was the moment chosen by the enemy to launch two offensives, that which we had to meet being in the Ypres Salient, and developing into the Second Battle of Ypres. As a historian of the war has pointed out, our troops fought against heavy odds. " A crushing artillery preponderance and the use of poison gas were more deadly assets than any weight of numbers. For days our fate hung in the balance, dispositions grew chaotic in the fog of war, and it became a soldiers' battle, like Malplaquet and Albuera, where rules and text-books were forgotten, and we won by the sheer fighting quality of our men." To add to our difficulties the operations at Gallipoli were proving costly in the extreme.

It was at this crisis that Lord Kitchener approached—among many other heads of municipalities—the Mayor of Deptford, Councillor W. A. Wayland, J.P. (as he then was: the Sir William of later days), with a request that he would undertake to raise a unit. We find " The Kentish Mercury " recording that at a meeting of the Deptford Borough Council on May 18th, 1915, the Mayor announced that he " had been asked by Lord Kitchener to do something more for recruiting, by forming either an infantry battalion or an artillery brigade. He had replied that he would use his best endeavours, and he appealed for the whole-hearted support of the Council in that direction."

The Council—we learn from the same source—approved a reply expressing confidence that Deptford, "recognising the gravity of the call," would do all in its power to raise a unit in record time.

The Hour had struck : the Man had come forward. The Other Men responded. At a town's meeting at the Deptford Town Hall on May 27th, 1915, the Mayor was able to announce that 200 men had already given in their names for the 174th Brigade. He also pointed out that " the voluntary system had failed to recruit the number of men necessary to ensure the successful termination of the war. It had failed because neither the Government nor the people had realised that they had to contend against and overcome a forty years' preparation by a nation numbering at the commencement of the war 70,000,000." The Rt. Hon. C. W. Bowerman, M.P., moved a resolution by which the meeting pledged itself to do all in its power to promote the formation and completion of the Brigade.

Recruiting offices were opened at the Town Hall, and there was a response which at times must have proved embarrassing to those engaged in the work. From Deptford, Brockley and New Cross they came : recruits of an excellent stamp : mechanics, shopmen, clerks and labourers, for the most part, of ages varying from 19 to 38. The neighbouring borough of Greenwich sent a goodly number of recruits, every whit as good as the men of Deptford. In six and a half days the fine total of 750 men had been attested ! The pledge which the Mayor had given on behalf of Deptford was nobly fulfilled : in six days— record time !—a Brigade was in being, and there was a large surplus of recruits who could not at the moment be detailed to a unit. In the rush of recruits during the first two or three days the Mayor, with the assistance of only one sergeant (one of experience and tact, be it said) was responsible for the maintenance of good order and discipline. It speaks volumes for all parties that the results were so satisfactory.

Major ﹍. R. Phillips, R.A., was gazetted to the command of the first Brigade formed—the 174th (Deptford) Brigade, Royal Field Artillery. The disused Thames Ironworks, in Blackheath Road, were taken over as headquarters, and no little ingenuity was exercised in adapting them to the business in hand. Energy and good will once again overcame difficulties which might well have been thought insurmountable, and in a surprisingly short space of time things were working smoothly.

" The Kentish Mercury " of June 11th, 1915, announced that the recruiting campaign in Deptford had been most successful, and that as a result two Gun Brigades—the 174th and the 179th—had been formed. " The men of the former" (the

2

writer stated) " have already been supplied with uniform. It is hoped that the 179th will be clothed in the course of next week." This was only a fortnight after the date of the town's meeting, and a good deal of firmness and an even greater measure of persuasive power must have been exercised by the Mayor of Deptford in inducing clothing contractors to deliver uniforms when their factories were working at such high pressure. It was done, however, and the hope expressed as to the 179th Brigade was also fulfilled.

Colonel D. Fulton, R.A., was appointed to the command of the 179th, and as there was again a surplus of recruits we find the Mayor, in " The Kentish Mercury " of June 18th, writing : " Your readers, I am sure, will be pleased to hear that the Secretary of State for War has placed in my hands the formation of a Divisional Ammunition Column, and I am hoping that I shall receive the enthusiastic support of the whole of Deptford in my endeavour to make another record for recruiting. We formed our 174th and 179th Brigades in a shorter time than any other borough." Once again the manhood of Deptford responded, and the Column quickly came into being. Lieut.-Col. A. E. S. Griffin was gazetted to the command.

The training of the 174th Brigade had so far progressed by June 24th—less than a month after it was opened for recruiting —that it could be inspected by Major-General Sir Francis Lloyd, commanding the London District. There were 760 of all ranks on parade, and their appearance justified the praise which they received. On July 15th Sir Francis Lloyd inspected 750 of the 179th Brigade, and again passed a warm encomium.

A further success was chronicled when, on July 23rd, 1915, the Mayor of Deptford wrote to the local Press : " I am pleased to inform you that we have recruited sufficient men for our 39th (Deptford) Divisional Ammunition Column, and we have thus completed the 174th and the 179th (Deptford) Brigades, R.F.A.—a total of 2,200 men in all. Feeling confident that Deptford men can still do better, I have consented to raise another Gun Brigade, which will be called the 184th (Deptford) Brigade, R.F.A., to give me the same enthusiastic support as they have given me in filling up the ranks of the other brigades."

Again was confidence justified, and by August 5th of that year a total of no fewer than 2,500 recruits were raised. When, on August 21, Sir Francis Lloyd carried out another inspection —in Deptford Park—the 184th Brigade (Lieut.-Col. C. M. Rudkin in command) and the 39th D.A.C. were on parade. A little later the 186th (Howitzer) Brigade was formed, Col. R. Oakes, R.A., being posted to the command.

It was a notable send-off which Deptford and Greenwich gave to the 39th (Deptford) Divisional Artillery on September 24th, 1915. A review was held on Blackheath, at which the Mayor of Deptford took the salute, and he might be pardoned if he felt a glow of pride as he surveyed the fine soldier-like body of men, in raising which he had played so conspicuous a part. After the review (which was filmed, and exhibited at home and in Allied countries) the Division left for Aldershot, there to be fitted for the strenuous task which lay before it. Allusion to this was made by the Mayor, in a valedictory address, which concluded as follows :—" I wish you all Godspeed and a safe return. Work hard and shoot straight ! Remember with pride the glories of the Royal Artillery !" How well the injunction was laid to heart this record will tell.

A correspondent of " The Kentish Mercury," who said of the parade it was " thrilling enough to revive the soul of a human slug," took farewell in the following words : " Their almost incessant tramping along a road not far from " The Kentish Mercury " office will be missed by those who, delighting in their youthful effervescent hilarity, learned to extol their virtues and excuse their faults, and they will dwell in our memories until the day arrives when we shall welcome them home again and congratulate them without restraint on their share in a triumphant victory."

Some notes on the professional side of the preliminary training will doubtless be read with interest :—

" Blackheath, with its beautiful turf in excellent condition, was adopted as the preliminary training ground, and marching and physical exercises were commenced with comparatively few instructors to impart the necessary instruction ; but amongst the recruits were a few ex-Army men who were able to fill the gaps and keep everyone on the move.

" Deptford in these days presented a very martial appearance with about 3,000 of its sons in khaki, and transport wagons laden with stores frequently passing through the streets.

" During the preliminary training period, the men were mostly billeted at their homes, or on householders in the surrounding districts.

" Many young officers joined the Divisional Artillery and were allotted to the various units.

" The duties to be learned by the young officers other than making themselves efficient " Gunners " were many. Only those who have had to endeavour to fathom the mysteries of a Pay and Mess Book, and all the vouchers relating thereto, can imagine what difficulties these youngsters were confronted with. The paying of billeting money to the various house-holders was a long, dreary task, and if successful in completing the duty without being out of pocket one was extremely lucky. There were occasions when recruits failed to answer their names at morning roll call, and the most successful method of dealing with such offenders was to regard the men as absent for that day, which resulted not only in the loss of a day's pay to the man, but also the loss of a day's billeting money to his worthy landlady.

" By adopting these measures the mothers of Deptford and district soon made it their duty to see that the lads in khaki billeted with them did leave their lodgings to attend parades as ordered, and the recurrence of cases of absence were few and far between."

Reference has been made to the whole-hearted way in which the Mayor of Deptford threw himself into the task of recruiting the detailed work in connection with which was admirably performed by Major Wilkinson. Clothing and equipment, too, presented innumerable difficulties. An even bigger job was to find horses, but before the Division left his Worship had got together more than 2,000 horses ! Unsuitable premises had been transformed into suitable ones for temporary barracks. In one other direction, too, the Mayor's untiring energy found an outlet. The War Office refusing, or being unable, to help, on him fell the responsibility of finding the requisite number—obviously a very large one—of junior officers. He scoured the country to get them—and got them of the right type !

A department in which his Worship received splendid backing was the keeping of the accounts. This work was undertaken by the Borough Accountant of Deptford (Mr. T. E. Charles), which is equivalent to saying that it was done as well as it could possibly be done. When the accounts were presented to the Paymaster-General that official spoke in highly complimentary terms of the way in which they had been kept.

Another who gave very valuable assistance in time of difficulty was Mr. A. Ll. C. Fell, the manager of the London County Council tramways, who, when the Mayor was in a quandary as to stabling the horses of the 137th (Heavy) Battery, R.G.A., placed the tramway stables in Evelyn Street at his disposal, and helped in every possible way.

Matter for congratulation is to be found in the splendid behaviour of the men during the months of their stay in the neighbourhood. Young soldiers of the very best character sometimes find the period of preliminary training monotonous, and get a little out of hand, but practically nothing of the sort was noted. There can be little doubt that the splendid response made by the borough to the Mayor's invitation to help in making the stay of the men a pleasant one, contributed in no small degree to this happy result.

In closing this section of the record it may be mentioned that the Mayor—he was still serving the office, with characteristic devotion to duty—renewed acquaintance with the Division. He visited these units, who greeted him with the enthusiasm reserved for a trusted and honoured leader.

TRAINING PERIOD

As soon as the Divisional Artillery was clothed and able to carry out dismounted drills, an inspection was made by Lt.-Gen. Sir Francis Lloyd at Blackheath, which was attended by all Batteries and Ammunition Columns. On the conclusion of the march past, General Lloyd complimented all ranks on the smart and very creditable turn-out and movements he had seen.

By this time a few horses had arrived for each unit, also a few ammunition wagons, which enabled riding and driving to be commenced, despite the fact that the majority of the animals were suffering from ringworm.

Guns and howitzers were the real need, the first instalment received in August being two 18 pdrs.; and, with the aid of dummy guns and ammunition wagons, gunners were instructed in the elementary details of gun drill. But " with or without drag-ropes prepare to advance " becomes, even to the most patriotic volunteer, pathetically monotonous, although on the other hand " prepare to mount " for gunners brought a vision of " trotting into action." It was a long, long while, however, before this vision was fulfilled.

The men were very patient under this monotony, but with the spirit of patriotism predominant, and every man a volunteer, such trials and troubles as gun drill with wagons or dummy guns, marching on Blackheath, the constant putting together of harness by one squad, and pulling it to pieces again by the next, seemed nothing so long as one was doing what was considered necessary to fit himself for the battlefield. All worked with a will, and many a smart young boy soon became a Bombardier on probation, and in a very short space of time Corporal or even Sergeant—a position which the " old contemptibles " could seldom reach without years of hard study and grind.

But this was war time, and very few of the " contemptibles " were available, so the young probationary non-commissioned officers worked and studied to do in a few months what generally took years for the regulars to do, and the success achieved in this respect alone was apparent by the lack of regular N.C.O.'s in the whole of the Divisional Artillery, in all but the senior ranks.

There was no shortage of talent amongst the recruits. Signallers, telephonists, shoeing-smiths, saddlers, farriers and fitters were practically all found from within the Division, sent on courses to be tested, and passed as qualified.

By the end of September units were ready to receive the remainder of equipment and remounts, and with the few guns in possession of each Brigade, moved into the Aldershot Command on 1st October, 1915, to settle down to training in real earnest, occupying barracks and hutments as organised units for the first time.

The training grounds and riding schools of Aldershot district soon began to reverberate with orders and commands in the dialect that can only pertain to men of Deptford.

From dawn to dusk they were hard at it learning the lessons as prescribed in that wonderful book, " Field Artillery Training," and also many lessons not so prescribed, but obtained from the book of experience.

Early in November rumours of another move were heard, which later on were confirmed, and the whole Divisional Artillery marched to MILFORD CAMP, near Godalming, to complete training and concentrate with the infantry they would later on be called upon to support in defence of their country.

To have the confidence of the infantry is one of the ambitions of all Gunners, and the Deptford Gunners had no mean task in this respect, as the Infantry were not Deptford lads, but entire strangers drawn from all parts of Great Britain ; but a perfect understanding was obtained at the time of concentration at Milford which remained throughout the whole war.

The march to Milford Camp. What a day ! Jibbing horses and teams, new harness temporarily fitted, recruit drivers, the majority of whom had never driven in a team before, and many other troubles occurred throughout the whole march, but the Divisional Artillery eventually did arrive at Camp, the last detachments of the D.A.C. arriving about 2 a.m. The many lessons taught during that day's march were never forgotten, and irksome as the march was, all ranks cheerfully lasted the course, which was a long one for partially trained men and practically untrained animals.

The march produced a few humorous incidents, one of the best being the wonderful foresight displayed by the cooks of the D.A.C., who, to ensure that they would be well provided with cooking utensils and equipment at Milford, practically stripped their cookhouse at Aldershot before leaving.

This fact became known when a very heavy marching-out damage bill was received, and all the missing articles were returned to Aldershot.

On the march many a groan was heard, and questions asked amongst the gunners as to " why the limbers were supposed to be seats for gunners if they could not have a ride," and also " what about the hours spent at drill with those limbers and wagons doing ' prepare to mount.' "

Arriving at Milford, units settled down very quickly, and training commenced in real earnest with the arrival of the guns, howitzers and remounts.

Christmas came all too soon. Those who were not fortunate enough to leave camp, celebrated the festive season in the usual Army way.

Milford Camp is not particularly pleasant at any time, and it was decidedly cold and wet in the winter of 1915-16. Gun drill, tactical exercises and full mounted parades in the wet and mud did not add to the joys of camp life, but all ranks felt that the time for leaving England was drawing near, so why worry about such trifles.

The conditioning of horses and mules of the Ammunition Columns was carried out daily, the " loads " on most days consisting of mud and manure which blocked the entrances to the horse shelters and stables, left by predecessors.

After very determined efforts the columns succeeded in removing this " legacy," with more benefits than " being able to get to the stables without floundering through mud " and " the conditioning of animals."

Still, with all the seemingly unsurmountable obstacles and difficulties, the gunners made progress, and towards the end of January, 1916, Brigades in turn proceeded to Larkhill Artillery Ranges to be tested as to their abilities in hitting dummy targets and other objectives, before proceeding to one of the theatres of war to take on targets of a more realistic nature. The shooting and manœuvres at Larkhill were good, all Brigades acquitting themselves with credit, and the 39th Divisional Artillery was pronounced by the inspecting officers as " fit for service overseas."

Musketry practices were carried out on return from Larkhill, and the balance of equipment available in England drawn from Aldershot Ordnance Depot.

Those who have known Milford Camp in mid-winter can fully appreciate the feelings of these gunners waiting to get off the mark, and for the final order " to mobilize."

At last mobilization was ordered, and the Division was going " somewhere."   Would it be France, Egypt, or where ?

But ere long all knew, and the departure from Milford will ever be remembered.   Entraining at Godalming in the frost and snow commenced on the evening of 2nd March, 1916—battery after battery, column after column departing at intervals each day until 8th March, when the last portion of the D.A.C. marched away, bidding farewell to the little tin huts which had sheltered them for a few months.

From the day the first recruit joined to the day of departure for France was about nine months, which, though perhaps not a record in itself, was certainly a determined effort on the part of all ranks to fit themselves in the shortest possible time to bear their part in the World War as representing the district of Deptford.

OFF TO FRANCE

Embarking at Southampton and landing in France at Le Havre caused very little difficulty.

The first days of units in the war area were :—

174th Brigade, R.F.A.	..	4th March, 1916.
179th Brigade, R.F.A.	..	5th March, 1916.
186th Brigade, R.F.A.	..	6th March, 1916.
184th Brigade, R.F.A.	..	7th March, 1916.
39th Div. Amm. Column	..	8th March, 1916.

After disembarkation, units proceeded to rest camps at Le Havre to await trains to convey them to a concentration area some 25 miles behind the British front line. The weather was as bad as it could be, snow and sleet fell, and it was bitterly cold ; but, once entrained, officers and men were able to snatch a few hours rest, which ended all too soon, the senior Brigade arriving at its detraining station early on 6th March, and marching to the concentration area—BLARINGHAM-LYNDE district—about 10 miles away, followed by the remainder of the Divisional Artillery as they arrived and detrained, the last portion of the Divisional Ammunition Column reaching the area on the 10th March.

The journey from Milford to the concentration area in France had its mishaps. Two men of the Ammunition Column of 174th Brigade were perhaps the most unfortunate by sustaining fractured legs, caused through a runaway team and wagon when about to entrain at Milford.

Many units were compelled to march to their billets in the concentration area during the night and in blinding snowstorms, but the marches were achieved without serious accidents occurring.

Oh ! those first billets in France.

Minds flew back to the first billets in England, and the landladies of Deptford.

Even Milford would be better than a cold cheerless barn with part of the roof off and possibly one side open to the elements ; but this was the war area, and only the beginning of the many discomforts our soldiers had to put up with.

The cooks proved themselves quite capable of turning out very appetising dishes from the ample supply of rations received, but the French beer was a long way from the standard and quality of that obtained in Deptford.

IN THE LINE

On the 7th March, 1916, orders were received that Brigades were to proceed to the forward area for attachment to units in the line for instruction.

174th Brigade proceeded to ESTAIRES on 9th March.

179th Brigade proceeded to ESTAIRES on 9th March.

186th Brigade proceeded to ESTAIRES on 12th March. and were attached to the 8th Divisional Artillery.

The 184th Brigade proceeded to STEENWERCK on 12th March, and were attached to 34th Divisional Artillery.

On March 21st instructions to form three Medium Trench Mortar Batteries arrived, these to be designated " X/39," " Y/39 " and " Z/39 " Trench Mortar Batteries.

Personnel required to form these new batteries were obtained from the Brigades and Columns of the Divisional Artillery.

The Brigades attached to the 8th Divisional Artillery were withdrawn from the line on 23rd March and joined their wagon lines.

The 184th Brigade, R.F.A., remained attached to 34th Divisional Artillery until 24th March

Brig.-Gen. R. W. Fuller, D.S.O., R.A., relinquished command of the 39th Divisional Artillery on 24th March, and was succeeded by Brig.-Gen. G. Gilson, D.S.O., from the Cavalry Corps.

On the 25th of March all Brigades of the Divisional Artillery were withdrawn from the forward zone and marched to the ST. VENANT area on conclusion of the first period of attachment for instruction.

The Divisional Artillery were then billeted as under :—

Headquarters 39th D.A. at ROBECQ.

174th Brigade, R.F.A., at MAZINGHEM.

179th Brigade, R.F.A., at BERGUETTE.

184th Brigade, R.F.A., at ST. VENANT.

186th (How.) Bde., R.F.A., at GUARBECQUE.

39th Divl. Amm. Column at BOURECQ.

During the period 26th March—1st April, units were busily employed in cleaning up, and obtaining stores and equipment still required.

On 2nd April the 174th and 179th Brigades sent a proportion of officers and gun detachments for a further period of instruction with the 33rd Divisional Artillery, the 186th Brigade sending personnel on 3rd April, and 184th Brigade detachments joined the 38th Divisional Artillery on 2nd April.

Major G. C. Dwyer, R.A., Brigade-Major, left the Divisional Artillery staff on being posted to the Heavy Artillery staff on 4th April, and was succeeded by Major Hon. B. J. Russell, D.S.O.

Lt.-Col. E. R. Phillips, 174th Brigade, left the Division on 11th of April, and was succeeded by Lt.-Col. J. G. B. Allardyce, R.F.A.

The attachment period came to a close, and the Divisional Artillery commenced the relief of the 38th Divisional Artillery in the FESTUBERT-GIVENCHY area on the 14th of April, the relief being completed by the 16th with the D.A. Headquarters at LOCON.

The Divisional Ammunition Column relieved the 38th D.A.C. at MOUNT BERNENCHON, and the whole Divisional Artillery were now " in action " under their own staff and commanders for the first time, ten months approximately from the day the first recruit joined at Deptford.

During the period of instruction in the line attached to other Divisions, the Divisional Artillery were very fortunate in having extremely few casualties, although the units to which they were attached came in for a considerable amount of hostile shelling.

Registration of the enemy's front line, machine gun emplacements and observation posts, and shooting at any visible working parties on the enemy's side of the line, were the chief targets engaged during April and May.

On 20th May, the Brigade Ammunition Columns were absorbed into the D.A.C., and the D.A.C. reconstituted into two Echelons.

The Brigades were reorganised into three 18 pdr. Batteries and one 4.5 Howitzer Battery per Brigade, the Howitzer Batteries being transferred from the 186th Brigade.

Several officers, N.C.O.'s and men joined during April and May. Lieut. O. C. K. Corrie, North Somerset Yeomanry, joined on 25th April, on appointment as Divisional Trench Mortar Officer.

As the result of an accident, Lieut. T. W. Coles, A/184th Brigade died on the 1st May.

During June, 1916, shooting similar to that carried out in May took place. Artillery preparation and support were given to the infantry in connection with a few successful raids against the enemy's trenches and other minor operations.

A larger operation was carried out by the Division against a portion of the enemy's trenches known as the BOAR'S HEAD on 30th June. The preliminary bombardment and wire-cutting by the artillery commenced on the afternoon of 29th, and was reported as very effective.

The final bombardment commenced shortly before 3 a.m. on the 30th, the Infantry going over the top just after 3 o'clock, the guns lifting their fire and putting down an intense barrage in strong support.

The enemy's support line which proved extremely difficult, was not reached by the Infantry, the German retaliation being most violent, even to the shelling of their own support trenches where we were endeavouring to gain a foothold.

The trenches penetrated were reported full of German casualties caused by our bombardment, over 20,000 rounds being fired by the guns during the operation. Eventually our Infantry evacuated the captured German trenches, and by about 7 o'clock the guns ceased firing.

On 8th July H.Q. Divisional Artillery moved to BETHUNE. During July several bombardments of the German trenches took place, in addition to the normal daily shoots previously planned.

A few batteries changed their gun positions during the month, in order to more effectively carry out special shoots, and towards the end of the month four batteries had been withdrawn from action to rest and for training.

The four months spent in this quiet sector were most instructive to all ranks, although no operations on a very large scale were undertaken.

In addition to the daily shooting, gun drill, laying and fuze setting took place, also building and improvements to gun positions.

In the wagon lines considerable work was carried out to improve the conditions both for men and horses.

Early in August the Divisional Artillery were relieved, and by the 10th all batteries were in the rest area.

On the 11th August the Division commenced its march to the south, concentrating at St. Michel, near St. Pol, for Brigade and Divisional training.

The three days' march were very pleasant, units bivouacking *en route*.

Training continued until the 24th August, when the Divisional Artillery marched to the BERTRANCOURT area, and on the 28th went into the line between BEAUMONT-HAMEL and the RIVER ANCRE.

During the period in the training area, Col. A. H. Carter, C.M.G., succeeded Lt.-Col. A. E. S. Griffin in command of the D.A.C., and Col. A. Eardly-Wilmot joined in succession to Lt.-Col. A. Kennard, D.S.O., 179th Brigade.

The Battle of the Somme, which commenced on July 1st, 1916, was continuing with varying success, the thunder of the guns being heard day and night without a break.

The entry into this area was to be the Division's debut in operations on a large scale, and all ranks were keen to prove themselves efficient and capable of fulfilling any task allotted.

Here we find beautiful undulating country with ripening crops glistening in the sunlight, and small villages almost hidden in the valleys. How different to the northern parts of the line !

Alas ! before the Divisional Artillery were due to leave, beauty had turned to desolation.

THE SOMME

At last the Divisional Artillery were to join in the great struggle taking place on the SOMME, the sector occupied being just north of the RIVER ANCRE, almost opposite the German stronghold of BEAUMONT-HAMEL.

BEAUMONT-HAMEL was very strongly held and fortified by the enemy, and up till now had successfully beaten off every attack made on its defences, although thousands of shells had been fired into it from the first day of the battle.

On September 1st an attack was made on the German trenches opposite, to assist a larger attack being made on the south of the river. The guns of the Divisional Artillery fired from 5 o'clock until mid-day, the German wire being well cut and the bombardment very effective. The batteries suffered few casualties, although they came in for a large amount of retaliation from the enemy's guns.

During September minor operations were undertaken against the enemy's trench system on the divisional front, also harassing fire on all the German communications.

On the 26th September the Division co-operated in the successful attack on THIEPVAL, and on the 28th in the attack on another German stronghold called the SCHWABEN REDOUBT. In this latter operation our infantry penetrated further into the enemy's lines than was arranged, but difficult as it was, owing to bad light and restricted observation, the guns were very skilfully handled with accuracy and rapidity, resulting in administering severe punishment to the enemy.

The success of this operation reflected great credit on the artillery observing officers and men serving the guns.

On the 29th the Germans heavily counter-attacked, regaining a part of the SCHWABEN, and in our attack on the 30th he was partially turned out again with considerable losses caused by gun fire.

The SCHWABEN was about the highest point the Germans retained in this area, and if it were lost the British would gain valuable observation of the enemy's lines, which was almost certain to affect future operations in the SOMME country. So the stout resistance offered by the Germans to every attack made on the SCHWABEN was quite anticipated.

During all the operations of September the Trench Mortars rendered invaluable assistance by engaging many strong points in the German front and support trenches, but the mortars came in for a great deal of enemy retaliation and suffered in consequence.

The wagon lines of the batteries and sections of the D.A.C. were very heavily worked during the month in keeping up the necessary supply of ammunition. Their hours were exceptionally long, as, for reasons of lack of water in the forward area, and less likelihood of casualties from the enemy long range guns—the whole countryside being one mass of horse lines—only a portion of the wagons and horses were kept in the forward area within about five miles of the guns, the remainder being sent back over fifteen miles to the rear.

Early in October several batteries moved to new gun positions in support of the successful attack on a part of STUFF TRENCH.

The Trench Mortars, strongly reinforced, carried out special operations and wire cutting in the vicinity of BEAUMONT-HAMEL on the 9th and 10th, firing over 3,000 rounds and causing considerable damage to the enemy's defences.

Twenty-two of the 48 mortars were put out of action mostly as the result of hostile shell fire, but the casualties to men were not too heavy considering the number and closeness of the mortar emplacements.

A great effort to complete the capture of the SCHWABEN REDOUBT was made on the 14th October, and, after hand to hand fighting, was successful, many prisoners being captured.

The operation was an extremely difficult one for the Artillery, as the greater part of the objective could not be observed from the observation posts. Added to this, the weather conditions made such observation as was possible most difficult, it being almost impossible for aeroplanes to render any assistance. The accuracy of the artillery fire again reflected very creditably on the F.O.O's and gun detachments.

Two abortive counter-attacks were made by the enemy on the 15th, and in response to S.O.S. signals of the Infantry, the Divisional Artillery barrage fire effectually caught the enemy's attacking troops, inflicting very heavy losses.

A similar counter-attack by the enemy on the 21st proved equally unsuccessful, and over 100 prisoners were taken.

The complete capture of STUFF TRENCH was effected on the 21st, and, observation being better than before, masses of the enemy were heavily shelled, causing many casualties.

By the last week in October the weather became so deplorable that operations had to be continually postponed.

The battle casualties during the month were not heavy, but owing to the wet weather and intense cold at night many cases of sickness, including eleven officers, had to be evacuated to the Base.

As in September, the supply of ammunition proved a very difficult operation. All known routes taken by our wagons at night were intermittently shelled by the enemy, and the tracks were pitted with shell holes, making it most unpleasant.

It was eventually decided to supply ammunition by day, moving across open country in small parties. This plan proved a great success, but the horses began to show signs of the hard strain they had been subjected to.

The whole front was fairly quiet until 13th November, when a large attack was made north and south of the RIVER ANCRE, in which the 39th Division took part.

The attack, timed to commence about 5.40 a.m., was most successful in spite of an exceptionally thick fog, and, by noon, BEAUMONT-HAMEL, which the Germans considered almost impregnable, having strongly resisted attacks extending over the last four months, and many other villages near by, were completely captured with hundreds of prisoners.

On the night of the 19th November the Divisional Artillery were withdrawn from action, having been continuously in the line since August.

The supply of ammunition for the operations in November could no longer be maintained by using wagons, as the going was too heavy and the distances too long. By means of improvised pack-saddles, eight rounds of 18 pdr. or four rounds of 4.5 inch howitzer ammunition were carried per animal, the animals being led by drivers on foot for the whole journey to the guns and back, and the cheerful spirit with which this arduous duty was performed by the long suffering drivers and horses deserved all praise.

On leaving the front the Corps Commander expressed his thanks to the Division for the excellent work performed during the recent operations, in the following terms :—

"Your Division is now leaving the Corps, and I wish to thank all ranks for the excellent work done since joining the Corps and taking over the line at the SCHWABEN REDOUBT down to the RIVER ANCRE. The Division has had a good deal of hard fighting, which has shown up the qualities of the Brigades and Battalions, the spirit and dash of the men being most conspicuous.

We shall always remember the gallant defence of the SCHWABEN REDOUBT, and the way the Division beat off counter-attack after counter-attack.

The captures on the 13th instant were a splendid feat, and a very fitting conclusion to the operations of the Division before leaving the Corps. The results will be far-reaching, not only on account of the number of prisoners and material captured, but on account of the damaging effect on the morale of the enemy.

Will you please tell all ranks of the Division that their work all through has been thoroughly appreciated, and that the departure of the Division is much regretted.

Success in war cannot be obtained unless all arms co-operate and work together in close combination. The many successes the Division has had is due to the untiring support given by your Artillery, which has never failed you. The calls on the Divisional Artillery have been heavy, but their response has always been prompt and efficient.

Will you kindly convey to all ranks of the gunners the thanks of the Corps for the efficient way they have ' played the game.' ".

An extract from another appreciation is as follows :—

" The Corps Commander wishes to thank Artillery Commanders responsible for the co-operation of the artillery on the 21st October, for the excellence of the arrangements made, and to congratulate all on the results obtained.

The whole action of the artillery reflects the greatest credit on all concerned, and speaks well for the high state of training and efficiency reached.

The infantry speak with the highest praise of the barrage which covered the attack."

A telegram was received from His Majesty the King by General Sir Douglas Haig after the operations on the 13th November, as follows :—

" I heartily congratulate you upon the great success achieved by my gallant troops during the past three days in the advance on both sides of the ANCRE. This further capture of the enemy's first line trenches under special difficulties owing to the recent wet weather, redounds to the credit of all ranks."

The gunners were extremely lucky throughout the operations from August to November in escaping with so few battle casualties, considering the many bombardments the gun positions and wagon lines received. Sickness caused much wastage amongst both officers and men, and when the time came to leave the SOMME area both men and horses were all but down and out.

After withdrawal from the line the Divisional Artillery were ordered to march north to the YPRES SALIENT—a place not yet known by many Deptford men.

On commencing the march it was found impossible for the horses to pull the wagons filled with ammunition, and the bulk of the shells had to be left at the nearest ammunition dump.

With lightened loads the march proceeded, but after two days it became imperative that both men and horses should receive immediate rest before continuing further. Two days' rest was granted, and the march resumed on 25th November— the Divisional Artillery eventually arriving in the back area of the SALIENT on the 28th for rest and refitting.

At the end of November the Divisional Artillery was reorganised into three brigades of six-gun batteries, and the 184th Brigade ceased to exist.

YPRES

The Divisional Artillery on arrival in the back area of the Salient had fourteen days' rest, but even this time was all too short for Commanders to do all they had planned, and an additional fourteen days would have been more than welcome.

With the transfer of Sections of 184th Brigade to the other brigades, the 184th Brigade became non-existent after nine months' active service in France. The bulk of the officers and men of the 184th were absorbed within the Divisional Artillery.

Inspections were carried out by Generals Plumer and Hunter-Weston whilst the Division was at rest, and several officers and men were sent on leave to England. Parties of officers and men had a look round the front line in anticipation of early occupation.

On 9th December the 179th Brigade proceeded into action in relief of a group of Belgian Artillery, and shortly after the 174th and 186th also moved into action, followed by the Trench Mortars to positions north of YPRES.

Shooting on strong points in the enemy's lines, and reprisals for hostile artillery fire, formed the bulk of the firing during December.

On Christmas Day a steady rate of fire was maintained throughout the day on the German front lines.

The New Year opened quietly, and considerable work was commenced on improvements to gun positions and wagon lines, adding to the comfort of both men and horses.

In the Honours Gazette of the New Year several officers and men were awarded decorations for valuable work on the SOMME and during the previous year.

The Divisional Artillery was further reorganised into two Brigades, and the bulk of the 179th Brigade left the Division to form an Army Brigade, the D.A.C. being formed into two gun ammunition sections and a section for small arm ammunition.

Capt. H. W. Wiebkin, Staff Captain, left the Divisional Artillery on appointment to Staff Captain of a Corps, and was succeeded by Capt. H. F. Burke.

In February, the weather became frosty, followed by heavy falls of snow. Several raids were carried out in which the Artillery co-operated.

19

On 20th February the Divisional Artillery were relieved in the line, and went back into Corps reserve, proceeding into action again on 1st March in the ZILLEBEKE sector.

During March there were no operations other than raids and retaliation shoots.

The D.A.C. were employed in the preparation of ammunition dumps and conveyance of material required for working parties building positions in the forward area, turning out on an average twenty wagons a day in addition to their other duties.

During April, co-operation in many raids on the German trenches was carried out with success.

On 10th April the 174th Brigade, Trench Mortars, and D.A.C. were withdrawn into reserve, and on the 20th, 186th Brigade were also in reserve, the 174th moving into the training area near the coast, the Divisional Artillery completing the month out of the line.

On 5th May, the 174th Brigade, having arrived from the training area proceeded into action followed by the 186th Brigade and the D.A.C.

On 17th May, Major Hon. B. J. Russell relinquished the appointment of Brigade Major, R.A., on appointment to command a Brigade, and was succeeded by Major M. E. T. Thorneycroft.

The greater part of the month was occupied in constructing battery positions for the forthcoming offensive, about fifty positions being under construction by working parties furnished from all units of the Divisional Artillery in addition to the normal duties of batteries and D.A.C. in the line.

During the first week in June the Divisional Artillery co-operated in two demonstrations against the enemy's trench system and batteries, especially during an attack made by troops on the right against WYTSCHAETE—MESSINES—and HILL 60.

C/186th were very heavily shelled and compelled to leave their position after having two gun-pits set on fire and ammunition blown up. Headquarters 186th were also bombarded on 28th, and during the night the Germans plugged in about 400 rounds of heavy howitzer shells. All other batteries received more than the usual amount of attention from the enemy, the D.A.C. and wagon lines being constantly shelled, causing many casualties to men and animals.

Early in July the 186th Brigade was withdrawn, having had a most unpleasant time for the past month. Headquarters 186th Brigade suffered another six hours' bombardment on the 3rd, about 600 shells being fired at their Headquarters.

By the 21st the 186th Brigade were again in action and the Divisional Artillery made preparations to participate in the great offensive about to be launched, known as the Third Battle of YPRES.

There were gun positions everywhere, and the guns appeared to be pointing in all directions which was more or less true.

Practice barrages were arranged and fired, the wagon lines and D.A.C. working unceasingly to maintain the supply of ammunition.

Just before 4 o'clock on the 31st July the attack commenced on the whole army front, and hundreds of tons of ammunition were fired.

For days the battle waged with varying success, all batteries firing in support intermittently day and night. Several batteries moved into advanced positions in and about the old British front line, where very little shelter or protection was to be found, the whole area being pitted with shell holes, gradually filling up with water.

The weather could not have been worse, but all ranks cheerfully responded to every call made in serving their guns under most trying circumstances.

Wagon lines and sections of the D.A.C. were shelled by day and bombed by night, giving practically no rest to either man or beast.

About the middle of July the Trench Mortars were equipped with new 6-inch mortars, giving a much longer range than their former weapons. The mortars were successfully engaged on wire cutting during the preliminary bombardment, and moved forward as progress was made in close support of the Infantry.

The battle continued during August, all batteries being engaged day and night in keeping the enemy's positions under continuous fire, and harassing his communications with shell fire, but although batteries were in very exposed positions which were heavily shelled on many occasions, there was no single instance of any battery failing to carry out its firing programme.

Many casualties were sustained during this period of the battle, and the work performed by parties delivering ammunition at all hours of the day and night thoroughly deserved the special merit received, the casualties to such parties being many.

By 23rd August the Divisional Artillery was withdrawn to rest and refit.

On September 1st, brigades moved into action again, and once more were engaged in harassing fire on the enemy's lines and positions, supporting minor operations in connection with the main objective.

The expenditure of ammunition was prodigious, but the supply was always equal to the demand. The chief difficulty was the actual conveyance to the gun positions.

In the forward area roads were practically non-existent, and, as on the Somme in 1916, pack transport was resorted to in addition to a system of light railways.

The main attack progressed slowly during September, the Divisional Artillery co-operating in all operations undertaken.

Hostile aircraft were very active, and paid nocturnal visits to the wagon lines and D.A.C. whenever night flying was possible.

By the middle of October the Divisional Artillery were withdrawn to rest.

Brig.-Gen. G. Gilson, commanding the Divisional Artillery relinquished the command on appointment to command the artillery of a Corps, having been in command of the Divisional Artillery since it landed in France, and was succeeded by Brig.-Gen. G. A. S. Cape.

By the 4th November all batteries were back again in action, continuing the harassing fire on the enemy's positions.

The areas occupied by the batteries were subjected to considerable hostile shelling, which caused many casualties.

On the 18th November the guns were withdrawn and the Divisional Artillery moved into the northern part of the YPRES sector.

Lieut.-Col. C. H. Kilner, commanding the 186th Brigade since the days of Milford Camp, was invalided to England at the end of November, being succeeded by Lt.-Col. G. S. Henderson.

Many of the officers and men were suffering from the effects of the continuous gas shelling they had been subjected to for the past month. Those affected were sent into the back area for rest.

On the 23rd November batteries moved into action in the PASSCHENDALE sector.

Lt.-Col. Lord A. E. Browne relieved Lt.-Col. Henderson in command of the 186th Brigade early in December, and Lt.-Col. J. G. B. Allardyce relinquished the command of the 174th Brigade on appointment to Royal Horse Artillery, being succeeded by Lt.-Col. E. W. S. Brooke.

By the middle of November the great battle had ceased except for minor operations in straightening out the line, and a continuance of harassing fire on all enemy movement day and night.

The enemy's artillery, during the whole time the Divisional Artillery were in this sector, carried out most intense shoots daily on the areas occupied by the guns, and the casualties to guns were numerous.

The ground in the vicinity of the battery positions was simply one mass of shell craters filled with liquid mud, and it was practically impossible to move a single gun from its position.

Thanks to the excellent " pill-boxes " the Germans had built during their occupation, the detachments had fairly good protection from shell fire and weather, but the conditions were so trying that detachments at the guns were relieved every forty-eight hours, much benefit being derived from the short spells of rest obtained in this manner, although the wagon lines were still subjected to periodical shelling by the enemy's long range guns. B/174th Brigade wagon line suffered thirty casualties to horses in one morning.

On the 22nd December the Divisional Artillery went into rest until 8th January, 1918.

During the November and December the D.A.C. were fully occupied in the salvage of ammunition, and also in removing derelict guns in the forward area caused through enemy shelling, and others being embedded fast in the mud and shell holes.

The trench mortar men assisted the D.A.C. in this work, and were instrumental in salving over fifty guns and thousands of rounds of ammunition.

Early in January, 1918, the Divisional Artillery moved into the forward area, but owing to recent heavy falls of snow, followed by a hard frost, the march was anything but pleasant on the slippery roads.

Several vehicles side-slipped into the ditches by the road-side, dragging the teams with them. Some units were only able to march half the arranged distance, being compelled to billet for the night and continuing the march next day.

The guns moved into action on the 8th, and on the 11th the Germans carried out a most intense bombardment of the area occupied by the batteries, firing about 5,000 shells of all calibres.

The casualties were slight in comparison to the volume of fire ; a few guns, however, were damaged.

Batteries withdrew from the line on the 23rd, and moved into the POPERINGHE area, in preparation for a rail journey to the southern part of the British front.

On arrival in the southern part of the line, billets were occupied in the BRAY area until 3rd February, when the 174th Brigade, D.A.C. and Trench Mortars moved into action, and the 186th Brigade commenced training.

On 18th February the 186th Brigade returned from training, relieving the 174th Brigade in action, who commenced training, the 174th moving into action again on 28th February, and the whole Divisional Artillery then co-operating in a raid on the enemy's trenches.

During February no large operations were undertaken, and the shooting was chiefly confined to engaging enemy movement and working parties, with much success. Hostile artillery was comparatively quiet in comparison with the shelling experienced while in the YPRES sector.

The D.A.C. were engaged in conveying ammunition and material to the forward area, and also in salvage work.

Enemy aircraft paid great attention to both the D.A.C. and battery wagon lines, causing many casualties.

March opened with the Divisional Artillery still in action holding the line, continuing harassing fire, raids, and destructive shoots on selected targets. On the 12th March they went into reserve, and to be ready to move at very short notice.

It was now practically certain that the enemy were about to attempt another great break through of the Allied front, but the actual place or places where the blows would fall were problematical.

In the opinion of many, the favoured spot would be the junction of the British and French Armies.

Whilst in reserve, the Divisional Artillery were extremely unfortunate in losing its Commander, Brig.-Gen. Cape, on the 18th March, who was killed whilst conducting a staff ride, and Lt.-Col. Brooke assumed temporary command.

THE GREAT RETREAT

At 4.30 on the 21st March the great blow fell on the front of the Fifth Army, of which the 39th Division formed a part. The bombardment and barrage were terrific, and by 10 o'clock the enemy had attacked in a thick mist on a front of about fifty miles.

From the opening of the bombardment the Divisional Artillery were " standing to," in reserve, and at 2 o'clock in the afternoon were ordered to reinforce the line, the enemy having succeeded in forcing back our forward positions.

On the 22nd the attack continued, and at 9 o'clock the 174th Brigade were ordered to withdraw, but, with the exception of " D " Battery, they were unable to get gun limbers to the gun positions, and therefore remained in action until the Infantry had withdrawn behind the guns, firing at such targets as it was possible to see.

Eventually the enemy worked round the flanks of these batteries, and were harassing them from flanks and rear with machine-gun fire. The detachments were withdrawn with sights and breechblocks, and sixteen 18 pdr. guns were consequently lost to the enemy. D/174th Brigade withdrew with its howitzers, came into action again, doing considerable execution against the advancing enemy with observed fire.

The 186th Brigade in the meantime, having their gun limbers close by, remained in action until the enemy were within 300 yards of the guns before withdrawing to fresh positions.

Two guns of C/174 in the workshop were obtained, and with four howitzers and guns of another brigade, engaged the enemy from new positions.

Tke attack still continued on the 23rd March, brigades withdrawing from time to time to new positions from which they were able to continue covering the retirement of the infantry, only moving back when compelled to do so by close enemy machine-gun fire, crossing the SOMME before the bridge was blown up. One gun of C/186 was destroyed by hostile shell fire.

Five guns of a battery which had become detached from its group were attached to 186th Brigade during the afternoon and a Heavy Battery attached to the Division from the early stages of the battle having suffered so many casualties, was reinforced by men from the 174th Brigade.

Advanced sections of the 186th Brigade did considerable execution to the enemy by occupying positions where direct laying and observation was possible.

On the 24th all batteries took full advantage of the many opportunities offered in engaging the advancing enemy with observed fire, and one section of A/186 did particularly good work over the open sights.

On an average 3,000 rounds per battery were expended against the enemy this day, and fire was maintained throughout the night.

All visible enemy movement was engaged on the 25th, but the targets were neither so plentiful nor in such vulnerable formations as on the 24th, and during the night all possible crossing places of the SOMME were kept under constant fire.

The retirement continued on the 26th, artillery support being rendered.

Brig.-Gen. W. G. Thompson joined, and assumed command of the Divisional Artillery, Lt.-Col. Brooke rejoining the 174th Brigade.

The Heavy Battery attached was transferred to its own Corps, having afforded most valuable covering fire and assistance whilst with the Divisional Artillery.

On the 27th March the enemy renewed the attack, the guns of the 39th Division engaging a part of the attacking troops with observed and barrage fire. The enemy, having forced back the right flank, compelled the 186th Brigade to withdraw to new positions, but before retiring the guns inflicted considerable losses on the enemy over the open sights. Several successful local counter-attacks were made during the afternoon under the personal direction of the Divisional Commander, artillery support being given.

During the evening, parties of the enemy crossed the Somme with machine-guns, placing some of the batteries in a somewhat exposed position.

On 28th March support and covering fire were given to what was known as CAREY'S FORCE—remnants of shattered units hastily collected under the command of General Carey—and at nine o'clock in the evening both artillery brigades reported that our infantry were retiring through the batteries, which, however, still remained in action, and were able to inflict considerable punishment on the enemy. The excellent work performed by A/186th, commanded by Major Turner, on the 28th March, was specially brought to notice.

The 174th Brigade withdrew during the night, after being shelled by a hostile battery almost from the rear, and the 186th Brigade supported a movement by CAREY'S FORCE, withdrawing on completion.

On 29th March the Divisional Commander, Major-Gen. E. Feetham, was killed whilst visiting the infantry, and Brig.-Gen. Thompson temporarily commanded the Division, Lt.-Col. Brooke again assuming temporary command of the Divisional Artillery.

Enemy movement was constantly engaged during the day, several batteries moving into fresh positions.

The 39th Divisional Infantry were withdrawn from the battle on the 30th March, and transferred to the northern part of the British front, Brig.-Gen. Thompson reassuming command of the Divisional Artillery, Lt.-Col. Brooke rejoining 174th Brigade.

Harassing fire was continued on 30th and 31st March.

The enemy opened a most violent bombardment in the early hours of the 4th April on a line just behind the battery positions, the range being gradually shortened until it came back on to our front line, and when the enemy's infantry attacked the shelling was again lifted to the area of the batteries. Soon after daylight the attack developed, the enemy succeeding in entering our front line. In the opening bombardment batteries suffered severely, some of the gun teams in positions near the guns being heavily shelled, and nearly all communications with observing stations and brigade headquarters were cut.

Battery signallers and telephonists did most excellent work in continually mending wires under very heavy fire in their endeavours to keep up communication, visual signalling being resorted to and maintained where possible.

A hostile attack, advancing in massed formation, was engaged with observed fire by C/186th and brought to a standstill.

The enemy attacking in great strength continued to push forward, but the batteries remained in their positions until nightfall.

A forward section of C/174 was reached by the enemy, but the two guns were recovered during the night.

The following report from a Heavy Artillery F.O.O. is an instance of the work done by the batteries :—

" Two hostile attacks developed about 4 p.m. and 4.45 p.m.

The advancing enemy were so heavily punished by the fire from the Field Artillery that they lost direction, and finally broke up and retired on both occasions."

As soon as the visibility admitted of the fire from the guns being observed by the observing officers, about 500 rounds per gun were fired into the enemy during the day.

Batteries having suffered heavy casualties—3 officers, 70 other ranks and 110 horses being either killed or wounded by shell fire and machine gun bullets—moved to new positions during the night.

The enemy did not resume the attack on the 5th, having evidently suffered most severe losses. A further change of gun positions was made, the Divisional Artillery now supporting Australian troops.

Both Brigades moved forward on the 6th to give better support to a proposed local attack being made the following day.

About 5 a.m. on the 7th an intense barrage was commenced in co-operation with an attack made by the Australians, causing considerable casualties to the enemy in addition to the capture of about 150 prisoners.

The 174th Brigade having been heavily shelled moved to new positions on the 8th, and on the 9th April the enemy once again shelled all communications and approaches to the battery positions with considerable effect, enemy infantry attacking about six in the evening, but the very heavy concentration of artillery fire brought to bear on the attack smashed it up.

Before dawn on the 11th a most violent bombardment again opened up on the battery areas, a considerable number of gas shells being fired, and the enemy once more renewed the attack. Severe fighting continued all day, batteries being able to employ a good deal of observed fire, causing much loss to the enemy's infantry.

The 39th Divisional Artillery were withdrawn from action on 13th April at dusk, moving to an area south of AMIENS in reserve and for refitting, being about the last of the troops who took part in the first day of the battle to be withdrawn.

During the whole period covered by this retirement the D.A.C. delivered ammunition to gun positions and small dumps to enable batteries to replenish their supply as required. Larger refilling points were established and maintained in rear by lorries attached to the D.A.C. Ammunition was also dumped at other selected places, so that a supply was immediately available at probable positions if and when the batteries further retired.

The daily average of rounds fired per gun was about 300, excluding April 4th, 9th and 11th, the D.A.C. handling approximately 100,000 rounds between March 21st and April 1st.

The Small Arms Ammunition Section of the D.A.C. on many occasions supplied the infantry with ammunition at battalion headquarters close to the front.

By May 1st the Divisional Artillery were back again in action under the Third Army, and early in the month special demonstrations were carried out by the Trench Mortars with 6-inch mobile (mounted) mortars.

A few raids also were carried out during the month.

On the 11th May the enemy carried out a concentrated bombardment with yellow gas shells, obtaining direct hits on the dug-outs of a detached section of D/174, resulting in the section moving the following day. B/174 also suffered in the bombardment.

On the 12th the S.A.A. Section of the D.A.C. was disbanded, also the Trench Mortar Batteries, leaving only a special detachment with the mobile mortars.

During June, raids and harassing fire continued, and by the 18th the 174th Brigade was withdrawn, followed by 186th on the 22nd, into reserve.

On the 25th the 174th moved into action from reserve, being relieved again on the 30th by a New Zealand Brigade, the 186th commencing mobile training.

During the last week in June No. 1 Section D.A.C. had an epidemic of influenza, and about 25 per cent. of the men were unfit for duty at one time.

The great German attack had failed in its attempt to reach the Channel ports and divide the Allied Armies. But at what a cost !

Miles of beautiful country were laid waste, with many towns and villages shattered almost beyond recognition.

It was the last chance which could possibly come to the enemy to effect the hoped-for break through, for his own resources in men and material, as well as supplies and animals, were at a very low ebb.

In the shock sustained by the British Armies with this supreme effort of the enemy, the 39th Divisional Artillery loyally and heroically took their share, adding honour to their name and also to the country and borough they represented.

But the enemy were now held in check, and with the advent of reinforcements the resumption of the offensive by the Allies was imminent.

On the 3rd July the Divisional Artillery was transferred by rail to Flanders to occupy reserve positions, the 186th Brigade subsequently moving into the line on the 7th, being relieved by the 174th Brigade on the 31st.

THE ADVANCE

On the 5th August the Divisional Artillery were withdrawn from the line and placed in G.H.Q. reserve, but proceeded into action again on the 15th for a special operation withdrawing on 21st, and on the 25th August it was transferred by rail from ST. OMER to the First Army, establishing Headquarters at AUBIGNY, wagon lines being located at ARRAS, ready to join in the further operations, which eventually terminated with the Armistice.

Guns were placed in position on the night 24/25th, and detachments withdrawn until late on the 25th, when the guns were manned, supporting an attack made by Canadian Infantry early on 26th August.

The attack was successful, the batteries advancing on 26th and again on 27th in close support.

Progress was made on 28th by the infantry under a creeping barrage of the artillery, several local counter-attacks made by the enemy being repulsed.

Further advances were made on 29th and 30th, the guns following in support, rendering assistance in repelling counter-attacks and harassing the enemy on all possible occasions.

Lt.-Col. Lord A. E. Browne, commanding 186th Brigade, was killed in action on 27th August, Lt.-Col. R. C. Reeves, joining on September 1st, taking over command of the Brigade.

The forward movement continued in September with the Divisional Artillery still in the line supporting the attacks of the Canadians, the majority of batteries having advanced sections ready to take on any fleeting target which presented itself, the opportunities being many, and full advantage was taken of them.

The enemy's guns and aircraft were very active against the areas occupied by the Division's guns and wagon lines during whole advance.

Another successful attack was launched by the Canadians on 26th September, both brigades supporting and advancing as the infantry made progress. Every opportunity was taken to inflict losses and damage to the enemy during the early days of October, and on the 9th both brigades assisted in the bombardment of the area near CAMBRAI, in support of an attack on the town, which was entirely successful, very little resistance being met.

The advance continued until the 19th, when preparations were made for another great attack. This attack was very successful, the guns moving forward according to the progress of the fighting.

On 25th October brigades were withdrawn to wagon lines into Corps reserve.

On 30th both brigades moved into action again and on 31st fired in support of the attack on VALENCIENNES, continuing the advance until 4th November, when the 39th Divisional Artillery were withdrawn and placed in Army reserve, where they were at 11 o'clock on the 11th November, 1918, when the Armistice was signed and the great World War came to an end.

It must be left to the great writers of the day to describe more accurately the feelings of our soldiers when the Armistice was signed and the World War brought to a conclusion. It is sufficient for this brief narrative to state that every one of the Deptford Artillery, from the highest to the lowest, were thankful the greatest struggle and slaughter the world has ever seen had come to an end, and that every call made on it had been responded to, thereby entitling the Deptford Artillery to rank amongst the victors.

TABLE OF UNITS

39th Divisional Artillery

HEADQUARTERS :—
> Formed at Aldershot 1st October, 1915.
> Disbanded 1919.

COMMANDERS :—

Brig.-Gen. C. GOULBURN	.. ..	From 1-10-15 to 1-3-16.
Brig.-Gen. R. W. FULLER	..	From 1-3-16 to 24-3-16.
Brig.-Gen. G. GILSON	.. ..	From 24-3-16 to 15-10-17.
Brig.-Gen. G. A. S. CAPE	.. ..	From 15-10-17 to 18-3-18.
Brig.-Gen. W. G. THOMPSON	..	From 26-3-18 to Demobtn.

174th BRIGADE, R.F.A.

> Formed at Deptford on 19th May, 1915.
> Equipment 18 pdrs.
> Taken over by Army 25th September, 1915.
> Embarked for France 3rd March, 1916.
> Disbanded 1919.

" A " Battery.—Remained as such until disbandment in 1919.

" B " Battery.—Became A/186th in 1916, disbanded in 1919.

" C " Battery.—Disbanded in 1916.

" D " Battery.—Became B/174th in 1916, disbanded in 1919.

Ammunition Column.—Disbanded on 20th May, 1916.

COMMANDERS :—

Lt.-Col. E. R. PHILLIPS	.. ..	19-5-15 to 11-4-16.
Lt.-Col. J. G. B. ALLARDYCE	..	11-4-16 to 17-12-17.
Lt.-Col. E. W. S. BROOKE	..	18-12-17 to 1-4-18.
Lt.-Col. F. E. SPENCER	.. ..	1-4-18 to Demobilization.

179th BRIGADE, R.F.A.

> Formed at Deptford on 3rd June, 1915.
> Equipment 18 pdrs.
> Taken over by Army 1st October, 1915.
> Embarked for France 4th March, 1916.
> Disbanded 30th January, 1917, on reorganisation of Artillery in
> France.

" A " Battery.—Became A/277 Army Bde., R.F.A., in 1917, and left
Division.

" B " Battery.—Became C/119 Army Bde., R.F.A., in 1917, and left
Division.

" C " Battery.—Became C/186 Bde., R.F.A., in 1916, disbanded 1919.

" D " Battery.—Became C/179 Bde., R.F.A., in 1916, disbanded 1917.

Ammunition Column.—Disbanded on 20th May, 1916.

COMMANDERS :—

Colonel D. FULTON	.. ..	3-6-15 to 5-1-16.
Lt.-Col. A. M. KENNARD	.. ..	5-1-16 to 11-8-16.
Colonel A. EARDLEY-WILMOT	..	11-8-16 to disbandment.

184th BRIGADE, R.F.A.

Formed at Deptford on 20th July, 1915.
Equipment 18 pdrs.
Taken over by Army on 1st October, 1915.
Embarked for France 6th March, 1916.
Disbanded 1st December, 1916, on reorganisation of Divisional Artillery.

" A " Battery.—Became C/174 in 1916. Disbanded in 1919.

" B " Battery.—Became B/186 in 1916. Disbanded in 1919.

" C " Battery.—Disbanded in 1916.

" D " Battery.—Became B/184 in 1916. Became C/186 in 1916. Disbanded in 1919.

Ammunition Column.—Disbanded 20th May, 1916.

COMMANDER :—

Lt.-Col. C. M. RUDKIN   ..   .. From 20-7-15 to 1-12-16.

186th BRIGADE, R.F.A.

Formed at Deptford on 21st August, 1915.
Equipment 4.5 Howitzer.
Taken over by Army on 1st October, 1915.
Embarked for France 5th March, 1916.
Disbanded 1919.

" A " Battery.—Became D/174 in 1916. Disbanded in 1919.

" B " Battery.—Became D/179 in 1916.

" C " Battery.—Became D/184 in 1916.

" D " Battery.—Remained as such until disbandment in 1919.

Ammunition Column.—Disbanded on 20th May, 1916.

COMMANDERS :—

Colonel R. OAKES	21-8-15 to 10-12-15.
Lt.-Col. C. H. KILNER	10-12-15 to 30-11-17.
Lt.-Col. G. S. HENDERSON ..	30-11-17 to 12-12-17.
Lt.-Col. LORD A. E. BROWNE ..	12-12-17 to 27-8-18.
Lt.-Col. R. C. REEVES	1-9-18 to Demobilization.

39th DIVISIONAL AMMUNITION COLUMN.

Headquarters and Nos. 1, 2 and 3 Sections.

Formed at Deptford 26th August, 1915.
Taken over by Army 1st October, 1915.
Embarked for France 7th March, 1916.
Reorganised 20th May, 1916, into " A " Echelon with H.Q., and 3 Sections and " B " Echelon.
Personnel, etc., of disbanded Brigade Ammunition Columns absorbed in Divisional Ammunition Column to complete to new establishment.
Reorganised into two sections and a Small Arms Section in January, 1917.
S.A.A. Section disbanded May, 1918.
Remainder disbanded 1919.

COMMANDERS :—

Lt.-Col. A. E. S. GRIFFIN	26-8-15 to 10-8-16.
Colonel A. H. CARTER	11-8-16 to 11-10-18.
Colonel F. W. BOTELER	13-10-18 to Demobilization.

TRENCH MORTAR BATTERIES.

X/39, Y/39, Z/39 (Medium T.M.).

Formed 21st March, 1916, in France, from personnel of Divisional
Artillery .
Equipment, 2 inch mortars. Re-equipped 1917 with 6 inch mortars.
Disbanded 1918.

V/39.   Heavy T.M. Battery.

Formed August, 1916.
Equipment 9.45 inch mortars.
Transferred to Corps 1918.

DIVISIONAL TRENCH MORTAR OFFICERS :—

Capt. O. C. K. CORRIE	..	..	From 25-4-16 to 1-6-17.
Capt. T. MULLIGAN..	..	..	From 1-6-17 to Demobtn.

Nominal Roll of Officers

39th Divisional Artillery

Lieut.-Col. J. G. B. Allardyce, C.M.G., D.S.O.
Lieut. G. L. Allen.
Major R. W. Allen.
Lieut. A. H. B. Anson.
2/Lieut. A. J. Applegate.
Capt. H. F. Burke, M.C.
2/Lieut. S. R. Barham, M.C.
Lieut. A. S. Barnes.
Lieut. H. F. Barnes, M.C.
Lieut. H. C. R. Butcher.
Major J. J. J. Bell, D.S.O., M.C.
Lieut. G. H. Barraud.
Major H. C. Baker, M.C.
Major F. J. L. Bennett.
Lieut. W. C. Bower.
Capt. R. E. Bowers, M.C.
Capt. A. Brown, R.A.M.C.
Lieut. L. B. Benny.
2/Lieut. P. P. Booth.
2/Lieut. A. N. Bradley.
Lieut. J. R. Blake.
Capt. E. Brinton.
2/Lieut. T. W. Borland.
Major V. S. Bland, M.C.
2/Lieut. H. P. Burnyeat.
Lieut. G. I. Bavin.
2/Lieut. G. H. Bartram.
Lieut. W. E. Bemrose.
Lieut. H. W. H. Beaumont, M.C.
Colonel F. W. Boteler, D.S.O.
Capt. E. C. Bevan, M.C.
Major N. M. de la P. Beresford-Peirse, D.S.O.
Lt.-Col. Lord A. E. Browne, D.S.O.
Lt.-Col. E. W. S. Brooke, C.M.G.
2/Lieut. A. S. Ball.
Capt. C. W. Care.
Lieut. T. W. Coles.
Lieut. E. F. Crowdy.
Major E. W. Clarke.
Colonel A. H. Carter, C.M.G.
Capt. G. L. Campbell.
Major K. H. Cousland.
Lieut. G. G. Cameron.
Lieut. R. C. Clancy.
Lieut. A. A. Campbell.
Lieut. H. S. Catling.
Lieut. W. E. Colesby.
Brig.-Gen. G. A. S. Cape, C.M.G.
2/Lieut. W. H. G. Compton.
2/Lieut. J. A. Casserley, M.C.

2/Lieut. R. M. Carse.
Capt. W. B. Carter.
Capt. O. C. K. Corrie, M.C.
Major G. T. C. Dwyer.
Lieut. C. B. H. Delamain, M.C.
Lieut. A. M. Diamant.
Lieut. W. S. Durward, M.C.
Lieut. A. W. Durrant.
Lieut. D. S. Doig, M.C.
Capt. W. I. Dill, R.A.V.C.
Lieut. G. M. Dodwell.
2/Lieut. F. W. Dewar.
2/Lieut. C. T. Doxat.
Capt. A. E. Delgado, R.A.M.C.
2/Lieut. H. R. Davies.
Col. A. Eardley-Wilmot, C.M.G.
Lieut. L. S. Edmonds.
Col. E. H. Eley, C.M.G., D.S.O., T.D.
Lieut. W. A. D. Edwards.
A/Capt. B. P. Evans.
Major A. H. Evans-Gwynne, D.S.O.
2/Lieut. S. E. Earle.
Brig.-Gen. R. W. Fuller, D.S.O.
Lieut. R. W. Follit.
Capt. H. L. Fitsell.
Capt. P. Filkins, M.C.
Major (T/Lt.-Col.) H. N. Fairbank, D.S.O., M.C.
Lieut. W. Fidler.
Lieut. W. H. Freeston.
2/Lieut. J. Fisher.
2/Lieut. S. W. Frearman.
2/Lieut. A. A. Field.
Colonel D. Fulton.
Lieut. H. H. Griffin.
Capt. O. A. Gamm.
Lieut. A. J. Gray.
Lieut. J. E. Griffith.
Lt.-Col. A. E. S. Griffin.
Capt. G. S. Goodall.
Capt. H. G. Garland.
Lieut. G. G. Game, M.C.
Capt. T. F. Gilkison, M.C.
Major J. A. W. Griffith, M.C.
Lieut. W. Garbutt.
Lieut. H. Gray.
Lieut. H. L. Green.
Lieut. D. G. S. Gregory.
Brig.-Gen. G. Gilson, C.B., C.M.G., D.S.O.
2/Lieut. H. W. Groves.
Brig.-Gen. C. Goulbourn, D.S.O.

Bt. Lt.-Col. H. K. HARLEY, D.S.O.
2/Lieut. G. S. HODGKINSON.
Capt. V. HILL.
Capt. A. C. HANCOCKS, M.C.
Lieut. D. G. HARRIES.
Lieut. H. J. E. HALL.
2/Lieut. A. HOE.
Lieut. H. J. HALL, M.C.
Lieut. W. H. HARDWICK.
Lieut. W. S. HUNT.
Lieut. H. B. S. HODDINOTT.
Lieut. J. HAITHWAITE.
Lt.-Col. G. S. HENDERSON.
Lieut. J. E. HENDERSON.
Major M. B. HEATH.
Capt. G. HERON, M.C.
2/Lieut. R. E. HUSTON, M.C.
2/Lieut. W. J. HORNER.
2/Lieut. R. A. HAYTHORNEWAITE.
Major I. W. L. JACKSON.
Lieut. E. V. JOHNSON.
Lieut. R. R. JEWELL.
Lieut. F. G. H. JOHNSON.
Lieut. D. M. L. JOHNSTON.
Major C. W. M. IVENS.
Major W. JONES, M.C.
Lieut. H. L. JUPP, M.C.
Lieut. H. W. JEFFRIES.
Lieut. L. H. JAQUES.
2/Lieut. D. G. JENKINS.
2/Lieut. E. W. IRVINE.
Lt.-Col. A. K. KENNARD, D.S.O.
A/Major E. C. R. KILKELLY, M.C.
Capt. G. C. KEMP, M.C.
Lt.-Col. C. H. KILNER, D.S.O.
Capt. S. B. KEKEWICH, M.C.
2/Lieut. B. R. KER.
Capt. D. E. KEMP, M.C.
Lieut. R. M. KING.
Capt. J. LAMB, M.C.
Lieut. S. E. C. LAMB.
Capt. C. LONGLEY, M.C.
Capt. A. M. LIVINGSTONE, M.C.
Lieut. B. V. LOVELOCK.
2/Lieut. F. G. LAWSON.
Lieut. H. L. LOWTON.
2/Lieut. L. G. LLEWELLYN.
A/Capt. J. LAMB.
2/Lieut. H. LUSCOMBE.
Lieut. C. K. MEDLIN.
A/Capt. W. C. McCAULEY.
Capt. D. J. MADELEY.
Lieut. O. N. MASH, M.C.
Lieut. W. E. MISKIN.
Lieut. A. J. MARRIOTT.
Lieut. R. A. MORRIS, M.C.
Lieut. W. J. MOSS.
Lieut. I. F. MACDONALD, M.C.

Lieut. R. H. MARRIOTT.
Lieut. R. H. MOULD.
Capt. R. W. MILES.
2/Lieut. R. A. McGOWAN.
Lieut. C. F. MANGIN.
Lieut. W. T. MILLER.
2/Lieut. A. MacNAB.
Lieut. H. S. MORLEY.
2/Lieut. J. MUIRHEAD.
2/Lieut. A. J. MacDUFF, M.C.
2/Lieut. J. R. MONTGOMERY.
Lieut. W. F. MEAD, M.C.
2/Lieut. S. H. MAXTED.
2/Lieut. D. MACPHERSON.
2/Lieut. E. V. MASON.
2/Lieut. R. A. MAYES.
2/Lieut. D. McCUNN, M.C.
2/Lieut. F. W. MILLWARD.
Capt. T. MULLIGAN, M.C.
Major W. S. NICHOLSON.
Lieut. W. NEILSON, R.A.V.C.
Lieut. G. E. NURSE, V.C.
2/Lieut. P. NEWHILL.
Lieut. H. M. OLIVER, M.C.
Lieut. F. D. ODELL.
Major R. J. O'CONNELL.
Lieut. J. N. OWEN.
Lieut. M. S. OXLEY.
Lieut. J. G. OLIVER.
Lieut. H. S. OTWAY.
2/Lieut. H. W. OAKHILL.
Colonel R. OAKES.
Lt.-Col. E. R. PHILLIPS.
Lieut. M. R. PITMAN.
Capt. W. PRATT.
Major C. C. PHILLIPS, M.C.
Major F. S. PERSHOUSE.
Capt. R. H. PORTER.
Capt. J. S. PRENTICE, R.A.M.C.
Lieut. J. E. S. PINCHING.
2/Lieut. H. E. B. PRATT.
2/Lieut. A. T. A. PRICE.
Major H. E. PITT.
Lieut. C. PHILLIPS.
Lieut. H. A. PAY.
Lieut.   B.   PENNEFATHER-EVANS,
    M.C.
2/Lieut. A. M. PRATT.
2/Lieut. W. PATCHETT.
2/Lieut. H. W. PEARCE.
2/Lieut. E. L. POWELL.
Major S. I. QUINN.
Capt. W. F. H. ROWE.
Lt.-Col. C. M. C. RUDKIN.
Major H. M. M. ROBERTSON, O.B.E.,
    M.C.
Capt. J. B. ROBERTON.
Capt. H. A. RAMSEY.

2/Lieut. P. C. RICHARDS, M.C.
Lieut. O. C. ROSSITER.
2/Lieut. R. C. RODGER, M.C.
Capt. W. B. REEKIE.
Lieut. W. F. RATTLE, M.C.
Lieut. F. R. RICE, M.C.
2/Lieut. R. RIPLEY.
Lieut. R. C. E. RANSOME.
2/Lieut. A. G. T. REES, M.C.
Capt. W. L. RILEY.
Lieut. D. L. ROBERTSON.
2/Lieut. J. H. ROBEY.
Major R. C. REEVES, D.S.O.
Capt. G. E. ROBINSON, M.C.
Lieut. W. D. ROCKLEY.
Major Hon. B. J. RUSSELL, D.S.O.
2/Lieut. E. B. ROBINSON.
A/Major K. O. SEIDLE, M.C.
Lieut. J. E. SIERRA, M.C.
Capt. A. D. P. SHARPUS.
2/Lieut. H. V. SEWELL.
Capt. F. H. STROUVELLE.
2/Lieut. A. SPRING.
Major W. STRACHAN, M.C.
Major (A/Lt.-Col.) F. E. SPENCER,
D.S.O., M.C.
Lieut. E. STRATFORD.
Lieut. L. STEPHENSON.
2/Lieut. F. STRAKER.
2/Lieut. G. L. STOKES.
Capt. J. V. SAUNDERSON.
Capt. H. J. SANDOM.
Lieut. G. R. SIMMS.
Lieut. H. C. SCHOLEFIELD.
Capt. J. E. SHEFFIELD.
Lieut. E. K. SMITH.
Lieut. E. P. SHANNON.
2/Lieut. D. STOCKDALE.
Capt. A. D. SOMERVAIL.
Lieut. J. W. STOBART.
Lieut. F. SHAW.
2/Lieut. C. SMITHER.
Lieut. P. Mc.D. SPENCE, M.C.
Capt. W. N. SODEN, M.C., M.D.,
R.A.M.C.
Capt. H. E. SWALLOW.
Lieut. A. K. STIRLING.
Capt. G. L. SALTON.
Capt. H. H. SLOANE, R.A.M.C.
Lieut. F. STEVENS.
2/Lieut. A. SINGLETON.
Lieut. L. G. SAMS.
2/Lieut. J. F. SOUTHAM.
2/Lieut. C. SIMPSON.
2/Lieut. R. J. SLATTER.
2/Lieut. G. D. SHAW, M.C.
Capt. G. I. THOMAS, D.S.O., M.C.
Capt. L. TALBOT.

Capt. J. D. TREMLETT, M.C.
Capt. T. B. THOMPSON.
Lieut. J. E. THOMPSON.
Capt. C. TURNER.
Lieut. J. B. THOMSON.
2/Lieut. A. TURNNIDGE.
Major G. F. B. TURNER, D.S.O.
Major M. E. THORNEYCROFT, D.S.O.
Major W. B. TELLING, M.C.
Lieut. F. S. TOCHER, M.C.
Brig.-Gen. W. G. THOMPSON, C.M.G.,
D.S.O.
Capt. F. J. TAYLOR.
2/Lieut. A. F. TURNER.
Lieut. C. G. VANDYKE.
Lieut. E. L. VALE, M.C.
Lieut. J. R. USHER.
Capt. H. W. WIEBKIN, M.C.
Major G. L. K. WISELY, M.C.
Lieut. L. F. WELDON.
2/Lieut. A. T. WILLIS.
Lieut. R. C. WEBB.
Major M. J. R. WOOD.
Lieut. E. S. WISE.
Lieut. R. O. B. WALPOLE.
Lieut. B. O. E. WALPOLE.
Major R. S. P. WELLS.
2/Lieut. C. A. WILSON, M.C.
Lieut. T. J. WILFORD, M.C.
Lieut. S. G. WIEBKIN.
Lieut. O. J. WOLSTENHOLME.
Major A. WITHAM, D.S.O.
Lieut. F. V. WALLINGTON, M.C.
Lieut. H. F. J. WADDINGHAM.
Capt. G. R. WATT, M.C.
2/Lieut. J. WENTWORTH.
Major J. E. WARNER, M.C.
Capt. S. L. WALL, A.V.C.
Capt. E. B. WHEELER.
Lieut. W. WINDOW.
Lieut. H. C. WARBURTON.
Lieut. V. WARDEN, M.C.
Lieut. C. H. WATSON.
Capt. W. D. WATSON, O.B.E., M.C.
Lieut. G. R. WHITE.
2/Lieut. F. WILDE, M.C.
2/Lieut. N. WALKER, M.C.
Major P. WRIGHT, M.C.
2/Lieut. G. G. G. WALKER.
2/Lieut. W. S. WALTER.
2/Lieut. A. WILCOCK.
2/Lieut. P. S. WILCOX.
2/Lieut. O. W. WILFORD.
Capt. W. WALE.
Major J. W. YOUNG, M.C.
Lieut. D. E. P. YOUNG.
Lieut. E. C. YATES.
2/Lieut. R. A. YOUNG, M.C.

CASUALTIES

OFFICERS
39th Divisional Artillery

RANK.	NAME.	NATURE OF CASUALTY.
Lieut. ..	STROUVELLE, F. H.	Wounded.
2/Lieut.	VANDYKE, C. G.	,,
Lieut. ..	COLES, T. W.	Died (result of an accident.)
2/Lieut.	STRAKER, F.	Died of wounds.
2/Lieut.	SIERRA, J. E.	Wounded.
2/Lieut.	GRIFFITH, J. E.	,,
2/Lieut.	SIMPSON, C.	Killed in action.
Lieut. ..	SHARPUS, A. D. P.	Wounded.
2/Lieut.	WISE, E. S.	,,
Capt. ..	BELL, J. J. J.	,,
Lieut. ..	HEATH, M. B.	,,
Lieut. ..	DURRANT, A. W.	Killed in action.
2/Lieut.	SEWELL, H. V.	,,
2/Lieut.	BOWER, W. C.	Wounded.
2/Lieut.	DIAMANT, A. M.	,,
Capt. ..	KILKELLY, E. C. R.	,,
2/Lieut.	BARNES, A. S.	,,
2/Lieut.	DOIG, D. S.	,,
2/Lieut.	BUTCHER, H. C. R.	,,
2/Lieut.	FREARNAN, S. H.	,,
Maj.(Bde.Maj.)	RUSSELL, Hon. B. J.	,,
2/Lieut.	EDMONDS, L. S.	,,
A/Major	KILKELLY, E. C. R.	Killed in action.
2/Lieut.	COMPTON, W. H. G.	,,
A/Major	KEMP, G. C.	Wounded.
2/Lieut.	WALKER, N.	,,
2/Lieut.	SLATTER, R. J.	,,
2/Lieut.	HORNER, W. J.	Died of wounds.
A/Major	TELLING, W. B.	Wounded.
2/Lieut.	MARRIOTT, A. J.	,,
A/Capt.	JONES, W. ..	,,
Lieut. ..	SIMS, G. R...	,,
2/Lieut.	EARLE, E. E.	,,
2/Lieut.	CASSERLEY, J. A.	,,
2/Lieut.	DIAMANT, A. M.	,,
A/Capt.	HEATH, M. B.	,,
2/Lieut.	RICHARDS, P. C.	,,
2/Lieut.	GRIFFITHS, J. A. W.	,,
2/Lieut.	BALL, A. S.	Killed in action.
2/Lieut.	PRATT, A. M.	,,
2/Lieut.	JOHNSON, E. V.	Wounded.
Major ..	WRIGHT, P.	,,
2/Lieut.	MAXTED, S. H.	,,
A/Major	STRACHAN, W.	,,
Lieut. ..	THOMSON, J. B.	,,
2/Lieut.	WILDE, F. ..	,,
2/Lieut.	LLEWELLYN, L. G.	,,

Appendix " C "—*contd.*

RANK.	NAME.	NATURE OF CASUALTY.
2/Lieut.	Shaw, G. D.	Wounded.
2/Lieut.	Macpherson, D.	,,
A/Capt.	Lamb, J.	,,
2/Lieut.	Carse, R. M.	,,
A/Major	Thomas, G. I.	,,
2/Lieut.	Patchett, W.	,,
2/Lieut.	Warner, J. E.	,,
Major	Spencer, F. E.	,,
2/Lieut.	Wilson, G.	,,
2/Lieut.	Griffiths, J. A. W.	,,
Major	Heath, M. B.	,,
Lieut.	Field, E. A.	,,
2/Lieut.	Walker, G. G. G.	,,
2/Lieut.	Walter, W. S.	,,
2/Lieut.	Llewellyn, L. G.	,,
2/Lieut.	Walker, N.	,,
A/Major	Quinn, S. I.	,,
2/Lieut.	Warner, J. E.	,,
2/Lieut.	Young, R. A.	,,
2/Lieut.	MacNab, A.	,,
Major	Wright, P.	,,
2/Lieut.	Mason, E. V.	,,
2/Lieut.	Groves, H. W.	,,
Lieut.	Johnston, D. M. L.	,,
Capt.	Delgado, A. E., R.A.M.C.	,,
Capt.	Hill, V.	,,
Capt.	Carter, W. B.	,,
2/Lieut.	Mayes, R. A.	,,
Major	Wright, P.	Killed in action,
2/Lieut.	Wilcock, A.	Wounded.
2/Lieut.	Wilcocks, P. S.	Killed in action.
2/Lieut.	Oakhill, H. W.	Wounded.
2/Lieut.	Wilford, T. J.	,,
2/Lieut.	Irvine, E. W.	Killed in action.
2/Lieut.	Robinson, E. B.	Wounded.
2/Lieut.	Haythornewaite, R. A.	,,
A/Capt.	Griffiths, J. A. W.	,,
2/Lieut.	Pearce, H. W.	Missing.
2/Lieut.	Newhill, P.	Wounded.
2/Lieut.	Powell, E. L.	Killed in action.
2/Lieut.	Carse, R. M.	,,
A/Major	Jones, W.	Wounded.
2/Lieut.	McCunn, D.	,,
A/Capt.	Crowdy, E. F.	,,
2/Lieut.	Wilford, O. W.	,,
A/Capt.	Carter, W. B.	,,
A/Capt.	O'Connell, R. J.	,,
2/Lieut.	Garbutt, W.	,,
A/Capt.	Wale, W.	Wounded. Subsequently killed by bombs whilst in Hospital.
A/Major	Siedle, K. O.	Ditto.
2/Lieut.	Morris, R. A.	Wounded.
2/Lieut.	Henderson, J. E.	,,

RANK.	NAME.	NATURE OF CASUALTY.
Major ..	CLARKE, E. W.	Wounded.
Lieut. ..	MASH, O. N.	Killed in action.
2/Lieut.	APPLEGATE, A. J. ..	Wounded.
2/Lieut.	LUSCOMBE, H.	,,
2/Lieut.	DAVIES, H. R.	,,
2/Lieut.	TURNER, A. F.	,,
2/Lieut.	BRINTON, E.	,,
2/Lieut.	WHEELER, E. B.	,,
Major ..	TELLING, W. B.	,,
2/Lieut.	WHEELER, E. B.	,,
2/Lieut.	BAVIN, G. I.	,,
Lt.-Col.	LORD BROWNE, A. E.	Killed in action.
Major ..	EVANS-GWYNNE, A. H.	Wounded.
2/Lieut.	ALLEN, G. L.	,,
T/Capt.	WELLS, R. S. P.	,,
2/Lieut.	BORLAND, T. W.	,,
2/Lieut.	RICE, F. R.	,,
2/Lieut.	RIPLEY, R.	,,
2/Lieut.	OLIVER, J. G.	,,
2/Lieut.	RATTLE, W. F.	,,
2/Lieut.	WILFORD, O. W.	,,
Major ..	FAIRBANK, H. N.	,,
2/Lieut.	WILSON, G. H.	,,
2/Lieut.	BRINTON, E.	,,
Major ..	TELLING, W. B.	,,
2/Lieut.	PRATT, H. E. B.	,,
2/Lieut.	PINCHING, J. E. S.	,,
Lieut. ..	ANSON, A. H. B.	,,
2/Lieut.	FIDDLER, W.	,,
A/Lt.-Col.	REEVES, R. C.	,,
Lieut. ..	WILSON, C. A.	,,
2/Lieut.	DEWAR, F. W.	,,
2/Lieut.	MILLWARD, F. J.	Killed in action.
2/Lieut.	McNAB, A.	Wounded.
2/Lieut.	MUIRHEAD, J.	,,
2/Lieut.	COLESBY, W. E.	,,
2/Lieut.	BLAKE, J. R.	,,
A/Major	PITT, H. E.	,,
2/Lieut.	RANSOME, R. C. E.	,,
A/Major	JONES, W. ..	Died of wounds.

CASUALTIES

39th Division (R.A. Headquarters).

RANK.	NAME.	NATURE OF CASUALTY.	DATE.
Gnr. ..	CAMPBELL, T.	Wounded	20– 6–17
Dvr. ..	ALDERTON, E.	,, ...	2– 7–17
Gnr. ..	KNIGHT, E. R.	,, ...	7– 9–18

179th Brigade, R.F.A.

Gnr. ..	HOGBEN, J. W. G.	Died (accidental) ..	7– 3–16
Dvr. ..	SMITH, J.	Wounded ..	10– 3–16
Dvr. ..	PRICE, S. H.	,, ...	14– 5–16
Gnr. ..	PATTEN, E. C. ..	Killed in action	17– 6–16
Gnr. ..	HITCHCOCK, W. H.	Wounded	17– 6–16
A/Bdr. ..	HOLMAN, A. A.	,, ..	4– 7–16
Dvr. ..	THOMAS, B.	,, ...	10– 7–16
Dvr. ..	TAYLOR, F.	Killed in action	17– 7–16
Gnr. ..	HARRIS, T. G.	,, ..	17– 7–16
Gnr. ..	TYLER, B. E.	Wounded ..	17– 7–16
Gnr. ..	LACEY, C. H.	Died (diphtheria) ..	23– 8–16
Gnr. ..	ARNOLD, J.	Wounded ..	3– 9–16
Gnr. ..	RAY, C. G.	,, ...	1– 9–16
Dvr. ..	HAMMOND, E.	Killed in action	3– 9–16
Dvr. ..	NOBLE, A. E.	Wounded ..	5– 9–16
Bdr. ..	MILLER, A. E.	,, ...	6– 8–16
Gnr. ..	BAKER, W. E. ..	Died of wounds	16– 9–16
Gnr. ..	COLE, A. H.	Wounded ..	16– 9–16
Gnr. ..	CAUGHLAN, S.	,, ...	14–10–16
Gnr. ..	BOWSTEAD, C. D. ..	Killed in action ..	20–10–16
Gnr. ..	PILCHER, S. G. ..	Died of wounds ..	21–10–16
Farr/Sgt. ..	MORRIS, J. ..	Died (Enteritis) ..	15–11–16
Gnr. ..	ASHELFORD, E. G. T. ..	Wounded ..	14–10–16
Gnr. ..	HALL, F. C.	,, ...	14–11–16
Gnr. ..	RANCH, S.	,, ...	6– 1–17
Gnr. ..	NORTH, H. W. ..	Died	9– 1–17
Gnr. ..	O'NEILL, W.	Wounded ..	14– 1–17
Gnr. ..	SULLIVAN, J.	,, ..	24– 1–17

179th Bde. disbanded on re-organisation, 30th January, 1917.

174th Brigade, R.F.A.

RANK.	NAME.	NATURE OF CASUALTY.	DATE.
Fitter	SMART, F. H.	Wounded	15– 4–16
Gnr.	BUTCHER, A. E.	,,	15– 4–16
Gnr.	NESBIT, J. G. W.	,,	19– 4–16
Gnr.	LANGRILL, J. W.	,,	19– 4–16
Corpl.	PARKER, W.	Died of wounds	16– 5–16
Gnr.	OTTY, J.	Killed in action	21– 5–16
Gnr.	HUNT, R.	Wounded	28– 5–16
Corpl.	CALLAGHER, L. C.	,,	16– 7–16
Gnr.	HUTCHINS, G.	Killed in action	10– 8–16
Sergt.	JOHNSON, F.	Died of wounds	7– 8–16
A/Bombr.	SMITH, W. H.	Wounded	10– 8–16
Gnr.	KING, W.	,,	10– 8–16
Gnr.	BUCK, J.	,,	10– 8–16
Dvr.	MOON, W. L.	,,	10– 8–16
A/Bombr.	CLARKE, C. J.	,,	15–10–16
B.S.M.	HINES, H. W.	,,	15–11–16
Gnr.	SAYERS, A. J.	,,	4– 9–16
Gnr.	SOUTHARD, C.	Died	31–12–16
Gnr.	BUCK, J.	Wounded	3– 1–17
Gnr.	GRANT, J.	,,	23– 1–17
Gnr.	LAITHWAITE, A.	,,	23– 1–17
Gnr.	PAYNE, A. E.	,,	23– 1–17
Gnr.	MANLEY, D. R.	,,	1– 2–17
Gnr.	WHYBREW, W. E.	,,	1– 2–17
Gnr.	MORRIS, A.	,,	1– 2–17
Gnr.	DAVIDSON, B.	Killed in action	31– 1–17
Gnr.	FEENEY, W.	Wounded	30– 1–17
Gnr.	BURROWS, W. W.	Died of wounds	1– 2–17
Fitter	ELLIOTT, B.	Killed in action	1– 2–17
Corpl.	SLOPER, R. J.	,,	1– 2–17
Gnr.	FORSHAW, E. H.	,,	1– 2–17
Gnr.	EAMES, G. R.	Wounded	8– 2–17
Gnr.	McNULTY, V.	,,	30– 1–17
Gnr.	EILES, W. J.	,,	10– 2–17
Sergt.	THOMAS, T. R.	,,	13– 2–17
Gnr.	GOBLE, L.	Killed in action	10– 2–17
Bombr.	BULL, E. E.	Wounded	17– 2–17
Gnr.	BAILEY, G.	,,	18– 3–17
Gnr.	JONES, R. E.	,,	8– 2–17
A/Bombr.	CASHIN, J.	,,	1– 3–17
Gnr.	ELLARD, G. C.	,,	1– 3–17
A/Fitter	LISTER, S. S.	,,	1– 3–17
Gnr.	LLOYD, P.	Missing	22– 3–18
Bdr.	BROSGARTH, W.	Wounded	4– 3–17
Gnr.	SIMMS, W.	Died of wounds	2– 3–17
Dvr.	REEVES, J. W.	Wounded	26– 3–17
Gnr.	REED, A.	,,	28– 3–17
Gnr.	HUSSEY, W.	,,	28– 3–17
Gnr.	CALLUP, W. J.	,,	28– 3–17
Dvr.	LUCK, F.	,,	9– 4–17
Dvr.	STRIVENS, E.	,,	9– 4–17
A/Corpl.	BURNETT, W.	,,	24– 5–17

RANK.	NAME.	NATURE OF CASUALTY.	DATE.
Gnr.	JAMB, H. J.	Wounded	24– 5–17
Gnr.	MARDLE, H. W.	,,	24– 5–17
Gnr.	COWDREY, E.	,,	26– 5–17
Gnr.	WILLIAMS, F.	Killed in action	24– 5–17
Sergt.	DUNFORD, J. W.	Wounded	26– 5–17
Gnr.	COX, A. J.	,,	4– 6–17
Gnr.	RODGERS, F.	,,	25– 5–17
Gnr.	RUSSELL, F. T.	,,	8– 6–17
Sergt.	VARNS, T. H.	,,	6– 6–17
Dvr.	HAWKINS, A.	,,	11– 6–17
Gnr.	McKINNA, C.	,,	10– 6–17
Gnr.	LEACH, F. J. M.	,,	14– 6–17
Fitter	SMART, A. W.	,,	16– 6–17
Bdr.	LUHMAN, F. C.	,,	20– 6–17
Bdr.	LYES, A. T.	,,	13– 6–17
Gnr.	AKEHURST, H.	,,	16– 6–17
Gnr.	SEABROOK, R. J.	,,	18– 6–17
Sergt.	WOOD, H.	,,	18– 6–17
A/Bdr.	NAYLOR, W.	,,	18– 6–17
Dvr.	HOGG, T.	,,	20– 6–17
Gnr.	McCULLOUGH, A.	,,	16– 6–17
Gnr.	ROFFEY, H. A.	,,	19– 6–17
Sergt.	FRICKER, F. E.	,,	20– 6–17
Gnr.	NIX, W. R.	,,	20– 6–17
Gnr.	WOOD, J. H.	Killed in action	19– 6–17
Gnr.	COX, A. J.	Died of wounds	20– 6–16
A/Bdr.	DALGARNS, J. S.	Killed in action	10– 6–17
A/Bdr.	WHITTAKER, C. L.	,,	10– 6–17
Gnr.	HUBBARD, A.	,,	10– 6–17
Sergt.	GREEN, C.	,,	9– 6–17
Fitter	SMART, A. W.	Died of wounds	17– 6–17
Gnr.	FORSYTH, F.	Wounded	4– 6–17
Dvr.	STOCKMAN, J.	,,	22– 6–17
Bdr.	DOHOO, H.	,,	21– 6–17
Gnr.	AUGUR, W.	,,	21– 6–17
A/Bdr.	PRENTICE, A.	,,	21– 6–17
Dvr.	PENDLEBURY, H.	,,	21– 6–17
Gnr.	BARRETT, M.	,,	21– 6–17
Gnr.	READ, A. L.	,,	21– 6–17
Gnr.	SHEPPARD, G.	,,	21– 6–17
Gnr.	CHALK, S. R.	,,	21– 6–17
A/Bdr.	PRENTICE, A.	Died of wounds	23– 6–17
Gnr.	FLYNN, J.	Killed in action	18– 6–17
Sergt.	Brady, H. E.	,,	22– 6–17
Corpl.	WHITTAKER, A. H.	,,	22– 6–17
Dvr.	RANDALL, A.	,,	22– 6–17
Gnr.	TRANTER, A. J.	Died of wounds	2– 7–17
A/Bdr.	AULD, G. F.	Wounded	24– 6–17
Gnr.	HAMILTON, J.	,,	25– 6–17
A/Bdr.	MARSHALL, J. H.	,,	25– 6–17
Sergt.	ABRAHAM, M.	,,	24– 6–17
Gnr.	SILVESTER, E. H.	,,	24– 6–17
A/Bdr.	BEECHEY, B.	Killed in action	6– 7–17
Gnr.	NEEDHAM, T.	Wounded	2– 7–17

RANK.	NAME.	NATURE OF CASUALTY.	DATE.
Gnr.	GATEHOUSE, D.	Wounded	29– 6–17
Dvr.	MESSIAS, R.	,,	2– 7–17
Gnr.	SMITH, H. E.	,,	7– 7–17
Dvr.	WITHERS, W.	,,	30– 6–17
Dvr.	BROGDEN, H.	,,	6– 7–17
Gnr.	ATKINS, E. C.	,,	10– 7–17
Gnr.	BAILEY, F. J.	,,	5– 7–17
Dvr.	WILLIS, J. W.	,,	6– 7–17
Dvr.	AINSCOUGH, J.	,,	6– 7–17
Dvr.	CARTWRIGHT, A. H.	,,	7– 7–17
Corpl.	BRAKE, P. H.	,,	17– 7–17
Gnr.	KEATING, J.	,,	17– 7–17
Gnr.	ATKINS, E. C.	Died of wounds	26– 7–17
Gnr.	MANLEY, D. R.	Killed in action	26– 7–17
Gnr.	JOKES, R.	,,	26– 7–17
Gnr.	ROBERTSON, E. J.	Wounded	25– 7–17
Corpl.	PERRY, F. W.	,,	24– 7–17
Corpl.	CARSTAIRS, J. L.	,,	24– 7–17
Gnr.	TOWNSEND, R.	,,	24– 7–17
Dvr.	SWOISH, C. S.	,,	24– 7–17
Sergt.	BREBNER, J.	,,	25– 7–17
Dvr.	JOYCE, P.	,,	25– 7–17
Gnr.	THOMPSON, G. M.	,,	26– 7–17
Dvr.	MCNULTY, V.	,,	26– 7–17
Dvr.	PAYNE, J.	,,	17– 7–17
Gnr.	MCDONALD, W.	Killed in action	25– 7–17
Gnr.	FLOWER, A. E.	,,	25– 7–17
Sergt.	BREBNER, J.	Died of wounds	3– 8–17
Dvr.	FELL, C.	Killed in action	31– 7–17
Sergt.	WATSON, B.	Died of wounds	4– 8–17
A/Bdr.	SPINNER, S. J.	Killed in action	31– 7–17
Sergt.	COTTER, G. A.	,,	3– 8–17
Sergt.	POULTER, N. H.	,,	3– 8–17
Dvr.	WARD, J.	Died of wounds	7– 8–17
Dvr.	TUDMAN, W. J.	Wounded	2– 8–17
Gnr.	PEARCE, E.	,,	2– 8–17
Gnr.	RINGER, T. G.	,,	3– 8–17
Gnr.	RUSSELL, J.	,,	30– 7–17
B.S.M.	HART, W. W.	,,	25– 7–17
Sergt.	BAMPTON, C.	,,	31– 7–17
Bdr.	MORLEY, W.	,,	31– 7–17
Gnr.	WINTER, B. J.	,,	31– 7–17
Gnr.	HIGGINS, W. H.	,,	31– 7–17
Gnr.	BRYANT, S. F.	,,	31– 7–17
Gnr.	DOBSON, P.	,,	31– 7–17
Gnr.	BROWN, G. A.	,,	31– 7–17
A/Bdr.	FLETCHER, H. W.	,,	31– 7–17
Gnr.	GRIFFEN, W.	,,	31– 7–17
Gnr.	GRAHAM, J.	,,	27– 7–17
Gnr.	MOLES, H. F.	,,	31– 7–17
Gnr.	MCBAIN, G.	,,	31– 7–17
Gnr.	BISHOP, H. L.	,,	16– 7–17
Gnr.	UNDERHILL, J.	,,	4– 8–17
Sergt.	ALGAR, T. C.	,,	3– 8–17

RANK.	NAME.	NATURE OF CASUALTY.	DATE.
Dvr. ..	SWINDEN, E.	Wounded	3– 8–17
Gnr. ..	ADAMS, F. T.	,, ...	4– 8–17
A/Bdr. ..	CHAPMAN, D. S.	,, ...	8– 8–17
Dvr. ..	SHORT, R. H.	,, ...	1– 8–17
A/Bdr. ..	MORTIMER, H.	,, ...	6– 8–17
Gnr. ..	RUTLAND, P.	,, ...	6– 8–17
A/Bdr. ..	KIRKHAM, J.	,, ...	6– 8–17
Gnr. ..	LATHAM, G.	,, ...	31– 7–17
Gnr. ..	PARKER, R. W.	,, ...	7– 8–17
Gnr. ..	MAXWELL, W.	,, ...	7– 8–17
Gnr. ..	WATSON, T.	Killed in action ..	8– 8–17
Sergt. ..	MERRITT, A. T.	,, ...	3– 8–17
Sergt. ..	GILL, F.	,, ...	3– 8–17
Sergt. ..	BARKER, D. E.	,, ...	6– 8–17
Gnr. ..	BUCK, S. G.	,, ...	3– 8–17
Dvr. ..	SEDDON, H.	,, ...	31– 7–17
Dvr. ..	LAWRENCE, E. D. ..	Wounded ..	6– 8–17
Bdr. ..	RUSHBROOK, E. T. ..	,, ...	15– 8–17
Gnr. ..	DAY, F.	,, ...	15– 8–17
Gnr. ..	RUSSELL, C.	,, ...	15– 8–17
Gnr. ..	TUCKFIELD, W.	,, ...	15– 8–17
A/Bdr. ..	FRENCH, F.	,, ...	15– 8–17
Gnr. ..	BURLEY, W. C.	,, ...	14– 8–17
Gnr. ..	ROFFEY, H. A.	,, ...	14– 8–17
Gnr. ..	WILSON, J. A.	,, ...	14– 8–17
Corpl. ..	HITCHMAN, A.	,, ...	13– 8–17
A/Bdr. ..	DAVIS, F.	,, ...	15– 8–17
Gnr. ..	GODWIN, S.	,, ...	15– 8–17
Gnr. ..	BUCK, J.	,, ...	15– 8–17
Gnr. ..	OGILVIE, A.	,, ...	14– 8–17
Gnr. ..	HAWKINS, P. A.	Killed in action ..	15– 8–17
Gnr. ..	HUMPHREYS, F. G. S. ..	,, ...	15– 8–17
Gnr. ..	MAW, A. W.	,, ...	15– 8–17
Gnr. ..	BRACEY, A.	,, ...	17– 8–17
A/Bdr. ..	LARD, E. D.	Wounded ..	25– 7–17
Gnr. ..	GLASS, T.	Killed in action ..	12– 8–17
Corpl. ..	MOTT, A. A.	Wounded ..	16– 8–17
Dvr. ..	BENNETT, E.	,, ...	16– 8–17
Gnr. ..	NICHOLLS, C.	,, ...	16– 8–17
Dvr. ..	GEORGE, J.	,, ...	20– 8–17
Gnr. ..	JEFFREY, H. T.	,, ...	19– 8–17
Gnr. ..	WALKER, E.	,, ...	21– 8–17
Bdr. ..	WELCH, H. W.	,, ...	19– 8–17
A/Bdr. ..	GREENER, J.	Killed in action ..	2– 8–17
Dvr. ..	LILLIE, D. E.	Wounded ..	6– 8–17
Gnr. ..	SHAKESPEARE, J. C. ..	,, ...	2– 9–17
Gnr. ..	LATHAM, F. G.	,, ...	3– 9–17
Gnr. ..	WALL, W. E.	,, ...	3– 9–17
Gnr. ..	SMITH-VERNON, E. ..	,, ...	2– 9–17
A/Bdr. ..	CROKER, F.	Died of wounds ..	12– 9–17
Sergt. ..	PULLEN, E. J.	Wounded ..	17– 9–17
A/Bdr. ..	CASHIN, J.	,, ...	20– 9–17
Gnr. ..	MOIR, D.	,, ...	20– 9–17
Gnr. ..	WEBSTER, H. M.	,, ...	20– 9–17

RANK.	NAME.	NATURE OF CASUALTY.	DATE.
A/Bdr.	Hopkins, W. P.	Wounded	20- 9-17
Bdr.	Spencer, H.	,,	18- 9-17
Gnr.	Randall, F.	,,	18- 9-17
Gnr.	Davey, H. A.	,,	18- 9-17
A/Bdr.	Sabiston, G.	,,	19- 9-17
Gnr.	Keeley, F.	,,	19- 9-17
Gnr.	Webster, J. A.	Killed in action	11- 9-17
Gnr.	Pearce, H.	Killed in action	11- 9-17
Gnr.	Robinson, A. J.	,,	11- 9-17
Cpl. (A/Sgt.)	Bond, H. J.	,,	15- 9-17
Gnr.	Trebble, F.	,,	19- 9-17
Gnr.	McVittie, —.	Wounded	5- 9-17
Gnr.	Grant, J.	,,	27- 9-17
Gnr.	Parker, G. R.	,,	25- 9-17
Gnr.	Bentham, J. J.	,,	25- 9-17
Gnr.	Arnold, C.	,,	24- 9-17
Corpl.	Benning, E. H.	,,	26- 9-17
Gnr.	Harper, T. R.	,,	26- 9-17
Gnr.	Carter, F. H.	,,	26- 9-17
Sergt.	Coleman, H.	,,	23- 9-17
Gnr.	Claxton, R. C. J.	,,	25- 9-17
Gnr.	Parker, R. W.	,,	25- 9-17
Gnr.	Cunningham, J.	,,	27- 9-17
Gnr.	Morris, A.	,,	27- 9-17
Gnr.	Sheldon, S.	,,	27- 9-17
A/Bdr.	Wright, A. R.	,,	19- 9-17
Gnr.	Moir, D.	Killed in action	20- 9-17
Gnr.	Toft, F.	,,	22- 9-17
A/Bdr.	Halden, J. J.	Died of wounds	26- 9-17
Corpl.	Morrow, F. R.	,,	27- 9-17
Gnr.	Weedon. J. D.	Killed in action	25- 9-17
Gnr.	Struchbury, F.	,,	26- 9-17
Gnr.	Grant, J.	Wounded	27- 9-17
Gnr.	Feeney, W.	,,	30- 9-17
Gnr.	Browning, R.	,,	25- 9-17
Gnr.	Panchen, S. C.	,,	24- 9-17
Dvr.	Latham, A.	,,	30- 9-17
Gnr.	McLaren, L.	,,	30- 9-17
Fitter	White, A.	,,	30- 9-17
Gnr.	Wheeler, A.	,,	30- 9-17
Gnr.	Gurden, C.	,,	30- 9-17
Gnr.	Munro, P.	,,	30- 9-17
Gnr.	Tait, R.	,,	30- 9-17
Corpl.	Watler, T. G.	,,	30- 9-17
Gnr.	Carr, A. G.	,,	2-10-17
Dvr.	Mishon, I. H.	,,	30- 9-17
Gnr.	Wood, J.	,,	30- 9-17
Gnr.	Smith, M. C.	,,	30- 9-17
Bdr.	Spurgeon, G. R.	,,	30- 9-17
Gnr.	Lloyd, P.	,,	30- 9-17
A/Corpl.	Brett, C.	,,	30- 9-17
Gnr.	Morrison, B.	,,	30- 9-17
Gnr.	Plummer, J.	Died of wounds	30- 9-17
Gnr.	Gemmell, J.	,,	30- 9-17

RANK.	NAME.	NATURE OF CASUALTY.	DATE.
Gnr.	Gale, A.	Killed in action	30– 9–17
Gnr.	Loades, H. P.	,,	30– 9–17
Gnr.	Pritchard, T.	Wounded	9–10–17
A/Bdr.	Wild, H.	,,	10–10–17
Gnr.	Marsh, A. N.	,,	10–10–17
Gnr.	Brown, C. L.	,,	6–10–17
Gnr.	Munro, P.	Died of wounds	5–10–17
Gnr.	Thomas, W.	Wounded	9–10–17
Gnr.	Turner, W.	,,	21–10–17
Gnr.	Samples, T. A.	,,	12–10–17
A/Bdr.	Glenister, F. J.	,,	6–11–17
Gnr.	Mills, C.	,,	6–11–17
Gnr.	Parker, G. R.	,,	6–11–17
A/Bdr.	Adams, W.	,,	6–11–17
Dvr.	Schofield, W.	Died	11–11–17
Gnr.	Walton, A. E.	Wounded	17–11–17
Gnr.	Wood, F. R.	,,	15–11–17
Gnr.	Moore, E.	,,	17–11–17
Gnr.	Palfreeman, H.	Killed in action	12–11–17
Gnr.	Lambert, C. G.	,,	12–11–17
Bdr.	Cadwell, G. T.	,,	17–11–17
Dvr.	Harris, A. H.	,,	17–11–17
Gnr.	Moreton, R.	Died of wounds	29–11–17
L/Bdr.	Roberts, W. A.	Wounded	18–11–17
Dvr.	Bowns, J. N.	,,	24–11–17
Gnr.	Coughtrey, T. G.	,,	19–11–17
Dvr.	Tims, F. G.	,,	17–11–17
L/Bdr.	Ware, G.	,,	22–11–17
Gnr.	Paxton, T. L.	,,	20–11–17
Gnr.	Pinder, G. H.	,,	20–11–17
Gnr.	Kinsey, G.	,,	18–11–17
Gnr.	Mayfield, S. R.	,,	30–11–17
Gnr.	Newton, W.	,,	19–11–17
Gnr.	Newman, M.	,,	19–11–17
Bdr.	Soloman, B. D.	,,	19–11–17
Sergt.	Lomas, T.	,,	22–11–17
Gnr.	Keyworth, M.	,,	22–11–17
Corpl.	Goodman, H. S.	,,	26–11–17
Dvr.	Ealham, S. G.	,,	27–11–17
Gnr.	Bentham, J. J.	,,	30–11–17
L/Bdr.	Weights, H.	,,	30–11–17
Gnr.	Murthwaite, W.	,,	20–11–17
Gnr.	Earp, F. A.	,,	24–11–17
L/Bdr.	Porter, A.	Killed in action	29–11–17
Gnr.	Lovell, H.	Wounded	26–11–17
Gnr.	Milby, J. H. T.	,,	21–10–17
Gnr.	Freeman, H.	,,	24–11–17
Gnr.	Bloor, G. E.	,,	26–11–17
Gnr.	Webber, A.	,,	25–11–17
Gnr.	Pearce, H.	,,	2–12–17
Gnr.	Ray, H. R.	,,	6–12–17
Dvr.	Stokes, W.	Died	7–12–17
Corpl.	Luhman, F. C.	Killed in action	6–12–17
Gnr.	Marsh, T.	Wounded	24–11–17

RANK.	NAME.	NATURE OF CASUALTY.	DATE.
Sergt.	ELLIOTT, W.	Wounded	21–11–17
Dvr.	CASTLER, T. J.	Died of wounds	10–12–17
Dvr.	JENKINS, T.	Wounded	10–12–17
Dvr.	HAINES, E.	,,	10–12–17
Gnr.	O'CONNOR, J.	,,	9–12–17
Gnr.	SEDGWICK, J.	,,	12– 1–18
Gnr.	BINNS, F.	Killed in action	12– 1–18
Gnr.	GREEN, J. F.	,,	12– 1–18
Corpl.	BRETT, C.	,,	12– 1–18
Gnr.	FRYER, C. W.	,,	12– 1–18
Gnr.	TAYLOR, E.	Wounded	11– 1–18
Gnr.	WILLIAMS, W. H.	,,	21– 1–18
Gnr.	QUINTON, W. A.	,,	23– 1–18
Bdr.	MILTON, E.	,,	21– 1–18
Gnr.	REAKES, E.	,,	21– 1–18
L/Bdr.	COOPER, A. T.	,,	27– 2–18
Gnr.	TURNBULL, N.	,,	4– 3–18
Gnr.	DRIVER, M.	,,	22– 3–18
A/Bdr.	PARTRIDGE, G.	,,	22– 3–18
Gnr.	GATEHOUSE, D.	,,	22– 3–18
Gnr.	GODWIN, S.	,,	26– 3–18
Corpl.	MACK, B. T.	Died of wounds	23– 3–18
Dvr.	DUCKWORTH, E. J.	,,	31– 3–18
A/Corpl.	ALMA, J.	Killed in action	4– 4–18
Sergt.	LEE, F.	Wounded	22– 3–18
Gnr.	HOLLANDS, A. R. J.	,,	29– 3–18
Gnr.	PROCTER, W.	,,	6– 4–18
Gnr.	JONES, W.	,,	4– 4–18
L/Bdr.	BUNKUM, R.	,,	4– 4–18
Sergt.	MATTHEWS, H. T.	,,	4– 4–18
Gnr.	MASON, T.	,,	4– 4–18
Gnr.	SMITH, L.	,,	6– 4–18
Gnr.	SCHOFIELD, W.	,,	6– 4–18
Sergt.	MAYHEW, H. J.	,,	6– 4–18
Gnr.	JORDAN, F. J.	,,	6– 4–18
S/S.	EDWARDS, E.	,,	31– 3–18
Dvr.	TOWNER, W.	,,	30– 3–18
Dvr.	POWELL, P. R.	,,	4– 4–18
Dvr.	ASHBY, W.	,,	4– 4–18
Gnr.	BROWN, C.	,,	4– 4–18
Gnr.	KETTLE, L. J.	,,	4– 4–18
Sergt.	ECCLES, R.	,,	Not known
L/Bdr.	SMITH, C.	Died of wounds	4– 4–18
Gnr.	JONES, W.	,,	5– 4–18
Gnr.	HAWKINS, W. A.	,,	5– 4–18
A/Corpl.	GEE, J.	,,	4– 4–18
Gnr.	WATMOUGH, W.	,,	9– 4–18
Sergt.	CRIPPS, E. H.	Killed in action	10– 4–18
Gnr.	RUSSELL, N.	,,	23– 3–18
Gnr.	WANNOP, S.	,,	23– 3–18
Dvr.	MAHONEY, A.	Died of wounds	11– 4–18
Dvr.	ANTRIM, A. C.	,,	10– 4–18
Corpl.	HATTON, F. J.	Killed in action	4– 4–18
Gnr.	McLAUCHLAN, H.	,,	4– 4–18

RANK.	NAME.	NATURE OF CASUALTY.	DATE.
Dvr.	VINSON, H.	Killed in action	28– 3–18
Dvr.	GEORGE, J. T.	Wounded	4– 4–18
Dvr.	QUINN, F.	,,	4– 4–18
Gnr.	LONGBOTTOM, F. R.	,,	4– 4–18
Gnr.	EVANS, A. J.	,,	10– 4–18
Gnr.	SLATER, J.	,,	11– 4–18
Gnr.	BUTCHER, W.	,,	6– 4–18
Gnr.	JACKSON, J.	,,	6– 4–18
Sergt.	ABRAHAM, M., D.C.M.,M.M.	,,	4– 4–18
Gnr.	WINTERS, H.	,,	4– 4–18
Gnr.	COLLIER, R.	,,	5– 4–18
Dvr.	WHITING, G. H.	,,	5– 4–18
Gnr.	BELL, J. H.	,,	9– 4–18
Corpl.	WALSH, T. M.	,,	12– 4–18
Bdr.	DAVIES, F.	,,	12– 4–18
Corpl.	DOWN, L. G.	,,	6– 4–18
Sergt.	DENISON, H.	,,	6– 4–18
Dvr.	WHITEHOUSE, F.	,,	6– 4–18
Corpl.	PENROSE, J.	,,	6– 4–18
Dvr.	WOOD, H.	,,	6– 4–18
Sergt.	COLEMAN, H.	,,	6– 4–18
Fitter	PARKER, T. H. J.	,,	4– 4–18
Gnr.	PRICE, W.	,,	10– 4–18
Dvr.	WADE, T.	,,	10– 4–18
Gnr.	MOYLE, T.	,,	12– 4–18
Gnr.	SHARP, J.	,,	4– 4–18
Bdr.	FRASER, W.	,,	4– 4–18
Dvr.	LINDSEY, E. J.	Killed in action	3– 4–18
S/S.	MIDDLEDITCH, E.	Wounded	10– 4–18
Dvr.	RENNIE, T. W.	,,	13– 4–18
Corpl.	MEDLEY, H.	,,	2– 5–18
Fitter	PARKER, T. H. J.	Died of wounds	9– 4–18
Gnr.	RUSSELL, J. W.	,,	18– 5–18
Gnr.	SLADE, P. A.	,,	9– 5–18
Gnr.	PREECE, T. W.	,,	10– 5–18
Bdr.	EDMONDS, F.	Wounded (Gas)	12– 5–18
L/Bdr.	READ, J.	,,	12– 5–18
Gnr.	CRAFTER, H. P.	,,	12– 5–18
Sergt.	MITCHELL, E. J.	,,	12– 5–18
Gnr.	OLIVER, G.	,,	12– 5–18
Dvr.	KENYON, W.	,,	12– 5–18
Gnr.	POTTER, J.	,,	12– 5–18
Gnr.	FRYER, C.	,,	12– 5–18
Gnr.	CATES, A.	,,	12– 5–18
Gnr.	LATHAM, F. G.	,,	12– 5–18
Bdr.	MILL, A. H.	,,	12– 5–18
Gnr.	ROBERTSON, E. J.	,,	12– 5–18
Gnr.	MEW, O. G.	,,	12– 5–18
Gnr.	EVERED, W. T.	,,	12– 5–18
Dvr.	DENNY, A. C.	,,	12– 5–18
Gnr.	SMITH, W. G.	,,	12– 5–18
Gnr.	OWEN, A.	,,	12– 5–18
Gnr.	THOMPSON, M.	,,	12– 5–18
Bdr.	BYOTT, F.	,,	12– 5–18

RANK.		NAME.			NATURE OF CASUALTY.	DATE.
Gnr.	..	PEGRAM, E. H.	..	..	Wounded (Gas) ..	12– 5–18
Gnr.	..	MILLER, C. R.	..	..	,, ..	12– 5–18
Sergt.	..	KIEFF, G. F. W.	..	..	,, ..	12– 5–18
L/Bdr.	..	BAILEY, F. J.	..	..	,, ..	12– 5–18
Gnr.	..	WILKINSON, G. A.	..	..	,, ..	12– 5–18
Gnr.	..	MURRAY, A. J.	..	..	,, ..	12– 5–18
Gnr.	..	PRAGNELL, L. C., M.M.	..	..	,, ..	12– 5–18
Gnr.	..	MOORE, L.	..	..	,, ..	12– 5–18
L/Bdr.	..	WELSH, W.	..	..	,, ..	12– 5–18
Corpl.	..	STEWART, J.	..	..	,, ..	12– 5–18
Bdr.	..	SMITH, L.	..	..	,, ..	12– 5–18
Gnr.	..	GILLIESPIE, J.	..	..	,, ..	12– 5–18
Gnr.	..	CULL, F.	..	..	,, ..	12– 5–18
Bdr.	..	STOKOE, J., M.M.	..	..	,, ..	12– 5–18
Dvr.	..	MAYNARD, G.	..	..	,, ..	12– 5–18
Gnr.	..	SHARP, J.	..	..	Wounded ..	12– 5–18
Gnr.	..	JONES, A.	..	..	,, ..	13– 5–18
Dvr.	..	CLARK, J.	..	..	,, ..	13– 5–18
Sergt.	..	HALLS, P. W.	..	..	,, ..	13– 5–18
Gnr.	..	SAUNDERS, J. R.	..	..	,, ..	14– 5–18
Gnr.	..	HUNTER, J.	..	..	,, ..	14– 5–18
Sergt.	..	ECCLES, R.	..	..	,, ..	15– 5–18
Gnr.	..	RUDDICK, G. H.	..	..	,, ..	15– 5–18
Gnr.	..	SHARP, J.	..	..	,, ..	15– 5–18
Sergt.	..	SIMPSON, W.	..	..	,, ..	4– 5–18
Sergt.	..	BERRY, P. W.	..	..	,, ..	9– 5–18
Gnr.	..	DUNMORE, A.	..	..	,, ..	11– 5–18
Gnr.	..	IBBETT, F. T.	..	..	,, ..	12– 5–18
Sergt.	..	LONG, A. T.	..	..	,, ..	12– 5–18
Bdr.	..	WETHERELL, A. J.	..	..	,, ..	12– 5–18
Gnr.	..	BIRD, W. J.	..	..	Killed in action ..	28– 5–18
Gnr.	..	BARTON, H.	..	..	,, ..	28– 5–18
Dvr.	..	DALBY, H.	..	..	,, ..	29– 5–18
Sergt.	..	HUBBLE, T. H.	..	..	,, ..	25– 5–18
Sergt.	..	SUMMERFIELD, P. J.	..	..	,, ..	26– 5–18
Dvr.	..	REED, A. C.	..	..	Wounded ..	14– 5–18
Gnr.	..	POOLE, H. P.	..	..	,, ..	25– 5–18
Gnr.	..	SHARPE, C., M.M.	..	..	,, ..	12– 5–18
Gnr.	..	SWAIN, E.	..	..	,, ..	14– 5–18
Gnr.	..	POTTER, G.	..	..	,, ..	16– 5–18
Gnr.	..	SCOTT, C. H.	..	..	,, ..	29– 5–18
A/Bdr.	..	VARO, E.	..	..	,, ..	29– 5–18
Gnr.	..	RIGGS, J.	..	..	,, ..	12– 5–18
Dvr.	..	BECKSON, P.	..	..	,, ..	31– 5–18
Sergt.	..	MURRAY, H., M.M.	..	..	,, ..	4– 6–18
Dvr.	..	ROOTHAM, F. C.	..	..	,, ..	1– 6–18
Gnr.	..	DARBY, H.	..	..	,, ..	9– 6–18
Bdr.	..	FRASER, W.	..	..	,, ..	15– 6–18
Gnr.	..	WHATTON, W.	..	..	,, ..	14– 6–18
B.Q.M.S.	..	BAGGALEY, H.	..	..	,, ..	14– 6–18
Sergt.	..	DENISON, H.	..	..	,, ..	14– 6–18
Gnr.	..	HUDDLESTON, A.	..	..	,, ..	3– 8–18
Gnr.	..	NOBLE, F.	..	..	,, ..	1– 8–18
Dvr.	..	DUNNING, A. E.	..	..	Died of wounds ..	27– 8–18

RANK.	NAME.	NATURE OF CASUALTY.	DATE.
Corpl	JEEVES, F., M.M.	Wounded	21– 8–18
Gnr.	TAYLOR, A.	,,	22– 8–18
Gnr.	STEVENSON, H.	Died of wounds	29– 8–18
Gnr.	GILMOUR, D. N.	,,	29– 8–18
Dvr.	PATRICK, W.	,,	2– 9–18
Gnr.	LAWSON, C.	Killed in action	4– 9–18
Dvr.	WILSON, J.	Wounded	27– 8–18
Gnr.	SPEAKMAN, A.	,,	29– 8–18
Gnr.	BAXTER, A.	,,	30– 8–18
Gnr.	SAVILLE, G.	,,	22– 8–18
Dvr.	SEAGERS, W.	,,	26– 8–18
Dvr.	HARRISON, J.	,,	30– 8–18
Gnr.	SMYTHE, H.	Killed in action	12– 9–18
Sergt.	LANGFORD, A.	,,	1– 9–18
Gnr.	STOCK, J. S.	,,	1– 9–18
Gnr.	GODDARD, R. W.	,,	1– 9–18
S.S.	HOLLAND, G. J.	,,	31– 8–18
Gnr.	SAUNDERS, J. R.	,,	5– 9–18
Gnr.	WILKINSON, A.	,,	5– 9–18
Gnr.	YARDLEY, F. W.	Died of wounds	2– 9–18
Sergt.	DENISON, H.	,,	1– 9–18
Gnr.	MUIR, J.	,,	8– 9–18
Dvr.	BREARLEY, F.	,,	11– 9–18
Sergt.	BARLEY, J.	,,	10– 9–18
L/Bdr.	WALLACE, A. V.	,,	12– 9–18
Gnr.	CHAPMAN, J.	,,	10– 9–18
Gnr.	AIREY, F.	Wounded	29– 8–18
L/Bdr.	SUTHERAN, G.	,,	30– 8–18
Sergt.	LAVERICK, J.	,,	31– 8–18
Gnr.	ROGERS, H.	,,	31– 8–18
Dvr.	LILLIE, D. E.	,,	31– 8–18
Gnr.	HAIGH, J.	,,	2– 9–18
Gnr.	USHERWOOD, F.	,,	3– 9–18
Gnr.	GARNER, L.	,,	4– 9–18
Gnr.	HARDY, J. W.	,,	4– 9–18
Dvr.	HAMES, A.	,,	5– 9–18
Bdr.	WILSON, J. R.	,,	1– 9–18
Gnr.	HALL, H.	,,	2– 9–18
Gnr.	ADDISON, T.	,,	2– 9–18
Fitter	ROGERS, F.	,,	3– 9–18
Dvr.	LEEDER, H.	,,	26– 8–18
Gnr.	BACK, C. M.	,,	7– 9–18
Gnr.	BURBAGE, A. C.	,,	7– 9–18
Gnr.	GRIFFITHS, F.	,,	7– 9–18
Gnr.	BROWN, C.	,,	7– 9–18
Gnr.	WILSON, J. A.	,,	1– 9–18
Gnr.	STRATTON, J.	,,	4– 9–18
Corpl.	WOODS, S.	,,	1– 9–18
Gnr.	SMITH, R.	,,	2– 9–18
Gnr.	ATTFIELD, W. A.	,,	2– 9–18
Gnr.	McGREGOR, P. S.	,,	7– 9–18
Gnr.	WHITE, E. F.	,,	7– 9–18
Gnr.	WINGATE, W. H.	,,	7– 9–18
Dvr.	DYER, H. J.	,,	7– 9–18

RANK.	NAME.	NATURE OF CASUALTY.	DATE.
Gnr.	PROUDFOOT, J.	Wounded	7– 9–18
Ftr/Cpl.	HANSON, T. J.	,,	7– 9–18
Dvr.	BENFORD, E. V.	,,	7– 9–18
Gnr.	TOOMEY, S.	,,	7– 9–18
Gnr.	SOMERS, H. G.	Wounded (Gas)	7– 9–18
Gnr.	McGURK, J.	,,	7– 9–18
Gnr.	WISE, S.	,,	7– 9–18
Gnr.	RHODES, F.	,,	7– 9–18
Corpl.	WILLIAMS, E.	,,	7– 9–18
Gnr.	BALFOUR, W.	,,	7– 9–18
A/Bdr.	KNIBB, C.	,,	7– 9–18
Sergt.	ROGERS, W.	,,	7– 9–18
Sergt.	PORTER, S. D.	,,	7– 9–18
Gnr.	WALKER, J.	,,	7– 9–18
Gnr.	PALLETT, G.	,,	7– 9–18
Bdr.	AVIS, E.	,,	7– 9–18
Bdr.	BLIGH, W.	,,	7– 9–18
Sergt.	PATTERSON, W. E.	Wounded	7– 9–18
Gnr.	MORGAN, R. C.	,,	8– 9–18
Gnr.	STUART, A.	,,	2– 9–18
Gnr.	TURNER, D. W.	,,	1– 9–18
Sergt.	ROBBINS, E. G.	,,	2– 9–18
Bdr.	SNOW, W. G.	,,	4– 9–18
Sergt.	SMITH, A. G.	,,	6– 9–18
Gnr.	HUNT, F. A.	,,	6– 9–18
Gnr.	SOMERS, H. G.	Died of wounds	16– 9–18
Gnr.	CALLUM, H.	,,	21– 9–18
Gnr.	SOUTH, G.	Killed in action	19– 9–18
Gnr.	MORRIS, W. C.	Wounded	5– 9–18
Dvr.	TRAINER, C.	,,	10– 9–18
Gnr.	GRAHAM, G.	,,	10– 9–18
Dvr.	HOLLAND, F. W.	,,	10– 9–18
Dvr.	KNOWLES, C.	,,	10– 9–18
Gnr.	MARTIN, R.	,,	11– 9–18
Gnr.	LLOYD, E. T.	,,	11– 9–18
Dvr.	WAINWRIGHT, A.	,,	27– 8–18
Gnr.	BROADLEY, R.	,,	14– 9–18
Dvr.	PATTEIN, J. T.	,,	14– 9–18
Gnr.	OSBORNE, W. R.	,,	14– 9–18
Gnr.	BAINES, E.	,,	10– 9–18
Gnr.	McLEOD, W.	,,	10– 9–18
Gnr.	WILKINS, T. H.	,,	12– 9–18
Fitter	BLACK, D.	,,	15– 9–18
Dvr.	STEWART, P.	,,	15– 9–18
Gnr.	HUMPHRIES, C.	,,	19– 9–18
Sergt.	BURDEN, E.	,,	19– 9–18
A/Corpl.	GILES, S.	,,	10– 9–18
Gnr.	HOLT, J.	,,	13– 9–18
Gnr.	McKENZIE, A.	,,	14– 9–18
A/Bdr.	EHRENFEST, R.	,,	16– 9–18
A/Sergt.	PENROSE, J., M.M.	,,	16– 9–18
Gnr.	WATTS, A. E.	,,	20– 9–18
Gnr.	ALLCOCK, T. J.	,,	20– 9–18
Dvr.	SHEEHAN, T.	,,	20– 9–18

RANK.	NAME.	NATURE OF CASUALTY.	DATE.
Bdr.	EALHAM, S. G.	Wounded	20– 9–18
Gnr.	PARRY, G.	,,	20– 9–18
Dvr.	MACK, J.	,,	19– 9–18
Gnr.	TINNAMS, B.	,,	19– 9–18
A/Corpl.	CAUSTON, G.	,,	18– 9–18
Gnr.	TAYLOR, J.	,,	6– 9–18
Gnr.	MARTIN, R.	Died of wounds	24– 9–18
Dvr.	TAYLOR, W.	,,	27– 9–18
Gnr.	TOWNSEND, J.	Wounded	17– 9–18
Siglr.	KINGSMAN, G. A.	,,	17– 9–18
Bdr.	SMITH, W. A.	,,	17– 9–18
Sergt.	MAILLARDET, W., M.M.	,,	19– 9–18
Gnr.	HOLLAND, W. F.	,,	18– 9–18
Gnr.	NEAL, J.	,,	16– 9–18
Gnr.	BURROWS, O. C.	,,	21– 9–18
Gnr.	SCOTT, C. H.	,,	21– 9–18
Gnr.	PRIESTLEY, C. W.	,,	26– 9–18
Gnr.	HIRST, J. L. C.	Died of wounds	29– 9–18
Gnr.	BYGRAVE, H.	Killed in action	28– 9–18
Dvr.	LORD, T.	Wounded	26– 9–18
Dvr.	SHAW, H.	,,	29– 9–18
Dvr.	HALE, F. C.	,,	27– 9–18
Gnr.	EAGLE, W. J.	,,	16– 9–18
Gnr.	SHACKLETON, R.	,,	17– 9–18
Dvr.	WILLIAMS, C.	Died of wounds	4–10–18
Gnr.	MANSELL, H. V.	Killed in action	3–10–18
Gnr.	RAYNER, E. L.	Died of wounds	8–10–18
Gnr.	PROCTOR, L.	Killed in action	6–10–18
Dvr.	WOOD, W.	Wounded	27– 9–18
Saddler	BAULCH, W.	,,	28– 9–18
Dvr.	DAVIES, B.	,,	28– 9–18
Dvr.	FOLKES, S.	,,	23– 9–18
L/Bdr.	PATIENT, G.	,,	26– 9–18
Dvr.	DIGNALL, R.	,,	28– 9–18
Wheeler	BAILEY, T. H.	,,	27– 9–18
Sergt.	BECKETT, E.	,,	30– 9–18
Sergt.	SMITH, A. G.	,,	5–10–18
Dvr.	MARCHANT, W.	,,	5–10–18
Dvr.	HARTLEY, H.	Died of wounds	16–10–18
Corpl.	GALLUP, W. J.	Wounded	7–10–18
Gnr.	QUARMBY, J.	,,	28– 9–18
Bdr.	QUARRINTON, T.	,,	28– 9–18
Dvr.	MALE, H.	,,	30– 9–18
Gnr.	KEDWARD, A.	,,	29– 9–18
Gnr.	HUGHES, T. J.	,,	13–10–18
Siglr.	MARSHALL, H.	,,	12–10–18
Dvr.	DOHERTY, W.	,,	13–10–18
Gnr.	DAVIES, E. W.	,,	13–10–18
Dvr.	FOWLER, W. G.	,,	13–10–18
Gnr.	WESTON, F. H.	,,	13–10–18
Gnr.	STAPLES, C.	,,	14–10–18
Dvr.	DIXON, W.	,,	14–10–18
Corpl.	SMITH, A.	,,	21–10–18
Gnr.	CADE, A. C.	,,	13–10–18

Appendix " D "—*contd.*

RANK.	NAME.	NATURE OF CASUALTY.	DATE.
Dvr.	SADDLER, J. H.	Wounded	13–10–18
Dvr.	HEAP, D.	,,	16–10–18
Gnr.	JONES, W. L.	,,	13–10–18
L/Bdr.	KNOCK, H.	Died (Influ. & Pneu.)	27–10–18
Dvr.	HOWLIN, J.	Wounded	13–10–18
Sergt.	BURNETT, W.	,,	13–10–18
Siglr.	PRICE, F. C.	,,	13–10–18
Gnr.	COWELL, S. E.	,,	13–10–18
Gnr.	LOVELL, W. H.	,,	13–10–18
Gnr.	TOWNLEY, R.	,,	24–10–18
Bdr.	SELL, G.	,,	13–10–18
Gnr.	TATTERSALL, A. R.	,,	13–10–18
Gnr.	BORKETT, T.	Died (Pneumonia)	4–11–18
Gnr.	JOHNSON, W.	Wounded	26–10–18
Gnr.	MILLS, H. A.	,,	24–10–18
Dvr.	GARNER, T.	,,	25–10–18
Sergt.	BISHOP, W.	,,	29–10–18
Sergt.	TERRY, A. J.	,,	29–10–18
Gnr.	DRURY, E.	,,	29–10–18
Dvr.	DYER, H. P.	Died of wounds	18– 9–18
Dvr.	ROBINSON, F.	Died (Influenza)	3–11–18
Gnr.	CARSLAKE, H.	Died (Pneumonia)	10–11–18
Dvr.	COOMBES, F. C.	Died (Influenza)	26–11–18
Sadd/Cpl.	GAWN, A. G.	Died (on leave)	24–11–18
Siglr.	THOMSON, H. R.	Died	25–11–18
Dvr.	O'CONNOR, D.	Died (Pneumonia)	10–12–18
Gnr.	GOODWIN, J.	Died	22–12–18
Gnr.	DIFFEY, G.	Died (Influenza)	20– 2–19
Dvr.	EMMOTT, J.	Died (Typhoid Fever)	28– 3–19

186th Brigade, R.F.A.

Corpl.	NORMAN, F. C.	Died	8– 7–16
Gnr.	MAULKIN, S. J.	Died of wounds	17– 7–16
Dvr.	CASTLE, F. W.	Wounded	17– 7–16
Gnr.	KING, W. E.	Killed in action	17– 7–16
Bdr.	JENKINS, W.	Wounded	17– 7–16
Gnr.	NEWTON, H.	,,	17– 7–16
Bdr.	RICHARDS, C.	Died of wounds	8– 8–16
Sergt.	BARRETT, F.	Wounded	7– 8–16
Gnr.	JOHNSON, F.	,,	7– 8–16
Bdr.	SMITH, J. H.	,,	1– 9–16
Bdr.	MACINTOSH, J. T.	,,	1– 9–16
Gnr.	WHIGHT, C. R. J.	,,	1– 9–16
Gnr.	MOFFETT, A. W.	,,	3– 9–16
Sergt.	BROWNE, B. W.	,,	9– 9–16
A/Bdr.	CHAMBERS, H.	,,	12–11–16
Gnr.	TAYLOR, A.	,,	7– 1–17
Gnr.	RROWN, W. A.	,,	20– 1–17
Gnr.	HOWARD, J.	,,	14– 1–17
Gnr.	DRUMMOND, W.	,,	27– 1–17

RANK.	NAME.	NATURE OF CASUALTY.	DATE.
Gnr.	QUEEN, A.	Wounded	27– 1–17
Gnr.	SINCOX, R.	Died of wounds	12– 2–17
Gnr.	MONCKTON, A.	Wounded	14– 2–17
A/Bdr.	BEASLEY, J.	"	11– 2–17
Sergt.	POWELL, W. A.	"	11– 2–17
Gnr.	DERBYSHIRE, T.	"	13– 2–17
Gnr.	WRIGHT, C. T.	"	13– 2–17
Gnr.	WHITLEY, F. A.	"	13– 2–17
Gnr.	WHITEHEAD, J.	"	13– 2–17
Sergt.	JONES, W.	"	11– 2–17
Gnr.	MARTIN, J.	"	17– 2–17
Gnr.	PHILLIPS, G.	"	15– 2–17
Gnr.	PERRY, J.	"	15– 2–17
A/Bdr.	FORSHAW, R.	"	15– 2–17
Gnr.	TRUSLOVE, T. A.	Killed in action	1– 3–17
Gnr.	WARNER, T.	Wounded	1– 3–17
Gnr.	HEDGES, P. H.	"	1– 3–17
Gnr.	SATCHELL, R. L.	"	1– 3–17
Gnr.	ARMFIELD, A. G.	Died of wounds	7– 3–17
Gnr.	PARKES, W. H.	Wounded	3– 3–17
Sergt.	KING, W. J.	"	21– 3–17
Gnr.	TANNER, J. A.	"	11– 4–17
Gnr.	SATCHELL, F. C.	"	31– 5–17
Gnr.	LOCK, C.	Died of wounds	9– 6–17
Corpl.	MUSTRE, H. G.	Killed in action	8– 6–17
Dvr.	CROSBY, W.	"	8– 6–17
Gnr.	HEARD,	"	7– 6–17
A/Bdr.	KEECH, A. J.	Died of wounds	11– 6–17
A/Bdr.	LEWINGTON, S.	"	12– 6–17
Dvr.	ELLIOTT, S. F.	Killed in action	8– 6–17
Gnr.	CAMPBELL, R.	Wounded	7– 6–17
Gnr.	NICHOLSON, E.	"	7– 6–17
Gnr.	HILL, S. E.	"	5– 6–17
Bdr.	PRESCOTT, J.	"	12– 6–17
Gnr.	PARISH, J. H.	Killed in action	20– 6–17
A/Bdr.	LEWIS, V. J.	Died of wounds	17– 6–17
Gnr.	NEWTON, F. C.	Killed in action	11– 6–17
Gnr.	PERRY, W. T.	Wounded	11– 6–17
Gnr.	WOOD, P. J.	"	11– 6–17
Gnr.	KIRKBRIDE, A.	"	12– 6–17
Corpl.	PRIESTLEY, A. R.	"	12– 6–17
A/Bdr.	CHAMBERS, H.	"	11– 6–17
S/S.	NAGLE, E.	"	12– 6–17
Gnr.	RODDIS, S.	"	20– 6–17
Gnr.	STONER, F.	"	18– 6–17
Gnr.	SOLLITT, H.	"	5– 7–17
Gnr.	WELLER, J.	Died of wounds	27– 6–17
Gnr.	BUTLER, G.	"	27– 6–17
Gnr.	LETTON, R.	Wounded	27– 6–17
Bdr.	KILSHAW, E.	"	4– 7–17
Bdr.	HOOK, H. S.	"	30– 6–17
Gnr.	McGOW, P.	"	27– 6–17
Gnr.	EVANS, J.	"	1– 7–17
Gnr.	GARMSTON, G. S.	"	

RANK.		NAME.			NATURE OF CASUALTY.			DATE.
Gnr.	..	PARKES, W. H.	..	..	Wounded	..	..	1– 7–17
Gnr.	..	DELIEU, W.	..	..	,,	..	..	1– 7–17
Gnr.	..	HILL, S. W.	..	..	,,	..	..	8– 7–17
Gnr.	..	MARCHANT, E.	..	..	,,	..	..	11– 7–17
Bdr.	..	SHIRLEY, R.	..	..	,,	..	..	13– 7–17
Gnr.	..	SUMMERS, W.	..	..	,,	..	..	13– 7–17
Gnr.	..	HENNESSY, F.	..	..	,,	..	..	13– 7–17
Gnr.	..	DRAPER, H.	..	..	,,	..	..	13– 7–17
Gnr.	..	PRYCE, R. S.	..	..	,,	..	..	14– 7–17
Gnr.	..	NEWLAND, E.	..	..	,,	..	..	14– 7–17
Gnr.	..	WHITE, P. W.	..	..	,,	..	..	13– 7–17
Gnr.	..	TUCKER, W.	..	..	,,	..	..	13– 7–17
Gnr.	..	SMITH, R. F.	..	..	,,	..	..	13– 7–17
S/S.	..	BROWN, W. G.	..	..	Died of wounds	..	..	25– 7–17
Gnr.	..	WALLER, S. W. J.	..	..	Wounded	..	..	30– 6–17
B.S.M.	..	LOW, G.	..	..	,,	..	..	25– 7–17
Gnr.	..	LANE, F. J.	..	..	,,	..	..	25– 7–17
Sergt.	..	IFOULD, F.	..	..	,,	..	..	25– 7–17
A/Bdr.	..	BAILEY, W.	..	..	,,	..	..	25– 7–17
Gnr.	..	MEAKIN, P.	..	..	,,	..	..	26– 7–17
Gnr.	..	SWETMAN, J.	..	..	,,	..	..	4– 7–17
Gnr.	..	HELM, G. M.	..	..	,,	..	..	22– 7–17
Gnr.	..	DITCH, E.	..	..	,,	..	..	22– 7–17
Gnr.	..	YONEL, J. W.	..	..	,,	..	..	22– 7–17
Gnr.	..	JONES, H. H.	..	..	,,	..	..	22– 7–17
Dvr.	..	NELSON, A. H.	..	..	,,	..	..	23– 7–17
Dvr.	..	SMITH, J. S.	..	..	,,	..	..	23– 7–17
Bdr.	..	PRITCHARD, P.	..	..	,,	..	..	23– 7–17
Gnr.	..	DIXON, A. G.	..	..	,,	..	..	23– 7–17
Corpl.	..	FLETCHER, H.	..	..	,,	..	..	28– 7–17
Dvr.	..	WILDING, S.	..	..	,,	..	..	28– 7–17
Gnr.	..	INKIN, S.	..	..	,,	..	..	29– 7–17
Bdr.	..	ROONEY, W.	..	..	,,	..	..	31– 7–17
Gnr.	..	FOLKARD, W.	..	..	,,	..	..	3– 8–17
Gnr.	..	KING, T.	..	..	,,	..	..	30– 7–17
Gnr.	..	CARVING, W. E.	..	..	,,	..	..	30– 7–17
Gnr.	..	LLOYD, D. U.	..	..	,,	..	..	29– 7–19
Gnr.	..	HOULDER, G. F.	..	..	,,	..	..	29– 7–17
Sergt.	..	BANKS, E. C.	..	..	,,	..	..	29– 7–17
Gnr.	..	SMITH, G. A.	..	..	,,	..	..	24– 7–17
Gnr.	..	HIRD, J.	..	..	,,	..	..	8– 7–17
Gnr.	..	HARRAWAY, A.	..	..	,,	..	..	1– 8–17
Gnr.	..	GODDARD, W. E.	..	..	,,	..	..	5– 8–17
Gnr.	..	MUSHAM, S. D.	..	..	,,	..	..	8– 8–17
Gnr.	..	CARTER, G. T.	..	..	,,	..	..	8– 8–17
Gnr.	..	CLARK, J. W.	..	..	,,	..	..	8– 8–17
Bdr.	..	JONES, A.	..	..	,,	..	..	10– 8–17
Gnr.	..	STYGALL, W.	..	..	,,	..	..	8– 8–17
Bdr.	..	HOLLAND, J. W.	..	..	Died of wounds	..	..	14– 8–17
Dvr.	..	FARMER, A.	..	..	,,	..	..	18– 8–17
Dvr.	..	PLUMMER, C. A.	..	..	,,	..	..	13– 8–17
Bdr.	..	QUEEN, A.	..	..	Killed in action	..	..	17– 8–17
Gnr.	..	SHELLY, A.	..	..	,,	..	..	17– 8–17
Gnr.	..	CHARLESWORTH, L.	..	..	,,	..	..	17– 8–17

Appendix " D "—*contd.*

RANK.	NAME.	NATURE OF CASUALTY.	DATE.
Gnr.	TAYLOR, L. F.	Killed in action	15– 8–17
Dvr.	WYTON, F. J. A.	,,	15– 8–17
Gnr.	JAGGER, S.	Wounded	12– 8–17
Gnr.	LOCK, J. G.	,,	12– 8–17
Gnr.	ASHFORTH, G. E.	,,	3– 8–17
Dvr.	ROBLEY, J.	,,	12– 8–17
Gnr.	STEWART, E. J.	,,	16– 8–17
Gnr.	HADEN, J.	,,	9– 8–17
Gnr.	HOWARD, J.	,,	13– 8–17
Bdr.	PETTIFER, L. J.	,,	13– 8–17
Dvr.	DUNN, T. W.	,,	13– 8–17
Dvr.	SAMUELS, J.	,,	13– 8–17
Farr/Sgt.	BARBER, R.	,,	15– 8–17
Gnr.	ROUND, L.	,,	16– 8–17
Sergt.	KNOTT, A. C.	,,	17– 8–17
Bdr.	CARTER, O.	,,	16– 8–17
A/Bdr.	GUTTERIDGE, E. H.	,,	16– 8–17
A/Bdr.	ODLIN, J.	,,	16– 8–17
Gnr.	CHEESEMAN, P.	,,	16– 8–17
Gnr.	CORBETT, A. H.	,,	9– 8–17
Gnr.	JANEWAY, J. F.	,,	13– 8–17
Gnr.	PAUL, A. J.	,,	13– 8–17
Gnr.	CHIVERS, J.	,,	15– 8–17
Bdr.	CONNELLY, J.	,,	15– 8–17
Gnr.	GROVES, A.	Died of wounds	19– 8–17
Gnr.	COWLES, M. W.	Killed in action	16– 8–17
Bdr.	BRIDGER, A. W.	,,	17– 8–17
Gnr.	GRAY, C. G.	,,	21– 8–17
Gnr.	MARKHAM, W.	,,	21– 8–17
Dvr.	ELLNER, W. E.	,,	21– 8–17
Dvr.	PACKER, P. L.	,,	21– 8–17
Dvr.	TAYLOR, W. B.	,,	21– 8–17
Dvr.	KILLINGTON, W. J.	,,	25– 8–17
Gnr.	CONSITT, J. A.	,,	21– 8–17
Gnr.	TANNER, J. A.	,,	16– 8–17
Gnr.	SMITH, J.	,,	18– 8–17
A/Corpl.	CLAY, T. C.	Wounded	17– 8–17
Dvr.	CROWTHER, W.	,,	16– 8–17
Dvr.	GREAVES, J. E.	,,	18– 8–17
Gnr.	STACEY, C.	,,	17– 8–17
Gnr.	EDGE, W.	,,	16– 8–17
Gnr.	HUNT, A. P.	,,	20– 8–17
Gnr.	JOHNSON, P.	,,	21– 8–17
Gnr.	MARTIN, W.	,,	21– 8–17
Gnr.	RAY, A.	,,	13– 8–17
Gnr.	MACFARLANE, C.	,,	16– 8–17
Gnr.	NEWLAND, H. F.	,,	18– 8–17
Gnr.	BUCKLAND, S. A.	,,	17– 8–17
Gnr.	ALBIN, A. V.	,,	21– 8–17
Gnr.	NORTHAM, S. R.	,,	16– 8–17
Gnr.	BLIGH, W. H.	,,	10– 8–17
Gnr.	PHILLIPS, G.	,,	16– 8–17
Bdr.	ELBOURNE, W. E.	,,	17– 8–17
Gnr.	HARCOMBE, H.	,,	20– 8–17

RANK.	NAME.	NATURE OF CASUALTY.	DATE.
Gnr.	BROOKS, F.	Wounded	20– 8–17
Bdr.	LAGDEN, A. W.	,,	21– 8–17
A/Bdr.	CAREY, R. G.	,,	19– 8–17
Gnr.	ABBOTT, W. H.	,,	22– 8–17
Gnr.	STYLES, J.	,,	22– 8–17
Sergt.	RODGERS, W. B.	Killed in action	17– 8–17
Gnr.	DICKINSON, A.	Died of wounds	19– 8–17
Gnr.	ORAN, F.	Killed in action	16– 8–17
Dvr.	GREAVES, J. E.	Wounded	17– 8–17
Gnr.	COX, A. E.	,,	12– 9–17
Gnr.	WILSON, B.	,,	12– 9–17
Gnr.	PARKER, G.	,,	12– 9–17
Gnr.	WHITESIDE, W.	,,	12– 9–17
Gnr.	MELLETT, J.	,,	12– 9–17
Gnr.	STAPLES, C. H.	,,	12– 9–17
Dvr.	HEDGER, J.	,,	11– 9–17
Dvr.	WELSH, C.	,,	11– 9–17
A/Bdr.	PARSONS, H.	,,	10– 9–17
Gnr.	BATTESON, A. J.	,,	11– 9–17
Gnr.	MARCHANT, W.	,,	12– 9–17
Dvr.	WANE, C. W.	Died of wounds	19– 9–17
Gnr.	WELLS, E.	,,	22– 9–17
A/Bdr.	McCOMISKEY, D.	,,	20– 9–17
A/Bdr.	BULL, A.	,,	20– 9–17
Dvr.	SMART, A. A.	Killed in action	19– 9–17
Fitter	WINN, E.	,,	17– 9–17
Gnr.	GIBSON, H.	Died of wounds	20– 9–17
Gnr.	WOOD, W.	Killed in action	27– 9–17
Gnr.	WRIGLEY, J.	Wounded	22– 9–17
Gnr.	STUBBS, B.	,,	20– 9–17
Gnr.	TYERNEY, W.	,,	17– 9–17
Gnr.	SWAN, W.	,,	13– 9–17
Sergt.	GIBSON, C. E.	Died of wounds	26– 9–17
Gnr.	ASHMORE, W. E.	Killed in action	1–10–17
Gnr.	WRIGHT, S.	,,	1–10–17
Dvr.	WILES, F. O.	Wounded	19– 9–17
Gnr.	WOOD, T.	,,	25– 9–17
Gnr.	GIBSON, J.	,,	29– 9–17
A/Bdr.	CAREY, J.	,,	23– 9–17
Gnr.	BULLIS, A.	,,	23– 9–17
Dvr.	ANGUS, T.	,,	20– 9–17
Dvr.	STREET, F.	,,	27– 9–17
Gnr.	COX, F. W.	,,	26– 9–17
Sergt.	HUGHES, W. E.	,,	30– 9–17
Gnr.	TINKLER, H.	,,	30– 9–17
Corpl.	DONALDSON, A. A.	,,	4–10–17
A/Bdr.	WRIGHT, W. R.	,,	29– 9–17
Gnr.	FENWICK, J. R.	,,	29– 9–17
Bdr.	LANG, G.	,,	1–10–17
Gnr.	PRATT, H.	,,	28– 9–17
Gnr.	RENNIE, C.	Died of wounds	1–10–17
Gnr.	MYALL, W. H.	Wounded	1–10–17
Gnr.	HARLOW, W. A. G.	,,	2–10–17
Corpl.	BEACH, B.	,,	3–10–17

Appendix " D "—*contd.*

RANK.	NAME.	NATURE OF CASUALTY.	DATE.
Corpl.	WHITNEY, G.	Wounded	1–10–17
B.S.M.	LOW, G.	,,	28– 9–17
Bdr.	HART, F.	,,	28– 9–17
Gnr.	BIRD, H.	,,	28– 9–17
A/Bdr.	MILNER, L.	,,	29– 9–17
B.Q.M.S.	FROUD, A. G.	,,	1–10–17
Sergt.	BELL, G.	,,	3–10–17
Gnr.	PARKES, G. C.	,,	3–10–17
Gnr.	STRICKETT, J. H. G.	,,	3–10–17
Bdr.	PAYNE, W. R.	,,	30– 9–17
Gnr.	HUNTING, J. W.	,,	3–10–17
Gnr.	SHOWBRIDGE, W. G.	,,	25– 9–17
Dvr.	GALLAGHER, P.	,,	26– 9–17
Gnr.	SMITH, G. H.	,,	26– 9–17
Gnr.	SHELDRICK, F.	,,	3–10–17
Gnr.	HAKE, S.	,,	1–10–17
Gnr.	COSTELLO, J. J.	,,	5–10–17
Gnr.	SATCHELL, E.	,,	23– 9–17
Sergt.	ARMES, C. G.	,,	12– 9–17
Sergt.	WILLETT, J. G. F.	,,	19– 9–17
Gnr.	EDWARDS, A. V.	,,	19– 9–17
Gnr.	KERSWELL, L. L.	,,	4–10–17
A/Bdr.	HAMLETT, W.	,,	7–10–17
Gnr.	NASH, A. W.	,,	10–10–17
Dvr.	TURNER, T.	,,	10–10–17
Dvr.	PARKER, J.	,,	10–10–17
Gnr.	McDADE, H.	,,	10–10–17
Gnr.	ASH, A. P.	,,	10–10–17
Gnr.	MEAKINS, T.	,,	3–11–17
Sergt.	MILLETT, J. G. F.	Died of wounds	6–11–17
Sergt.	BATT, H. J.	Wounded	5–11–17
Gnr.	ANGUS, W. A.	,,	10–11–17
A/Bdr.	DYE, J.	,,	8–11–17
Gnr.	LAWTON, F.	,,	6–11–17
Gnr.	MARSHALL, G.	,,	9–11–17
Gnr.	BURTON, E.	,,	7–11–17
A/Bdr.	BRACKLEY, W.	,,	8–10–17
Sergt.	JONES, W.	,,	12–11–17
Gnr.	FULLER, R.	,,	12–11–17
Gnr.	COURSE, J.	,,	16–11–17
Gnr.	MATTHEWS, S.	,,	15–11–17
Gnr.	HAYDOCK, T. H.	,,	18–11–17
Gnr.	FELLS, A. J.	,,	16–11–17
L/Bdr.	DELIEU, T.	,,	17–11–17
Gnr.	COFFEY, T.	,,	19–11–17
A/Bdr.	ODLIN, J.	,,	19–11–17
Gnr.	ECROYD, W. H.	,,	19–11–17
Gnr.	MOSCROP, J. A.	,,	18–11–17
Gnr.	HALL, H.	,,	18–11–17
Sergt.	ADAMS, W. H.	,,	20–11–17
Bdr.	ALLEN, W.	,,	20–11–17
Sergt.	MONTEITH, J. B.	,,	20–11–17
Gnr.	NOCKS, T. E.	,,	20–11–17
Gnr.	CLARK, G.	,,	20–11–17

60

RANK.	NAME.	NATURE OF CASUALTY.	DATE.
Gnr.	RYCROFT, R. H.	Wounded	20–11–17
Gnr.	GARLAND, H. J.	,,	20–11–17
Gnr.	PRESTON, H.	,,	20–11–17
Gnr.	MARSDEN, L.	,,	20–11–17
L/Bdr.	GREGORY, T. H.	,,	20–11–17
Gnr.	GREEN, H. J.	,,	20–11–17
Gnr.	HEXTER, A. E.	,,	20–11–17
Bdr.	KIPLING, W.	,,	20–11–17
L/Bdr.	HOLLAND, A. H.	,,	20–11–17
Gnr.	WHITEHEAD, H.	,,	20–11–17
Gnr.	WHELAN, J.	,,	20–11–17
Sergt.	DAVIS, L. A.	,,	20–11–17
Gnr.	OSBORNE, H.	,,	20–11–17
Gnr.	GELDARD, E.	,,	20–11–17
Dvr.	VINCENT, J.	,,	20–11–17
Gnr.	NIELD, S.	,,	20–11–17
Gnr.	HARRIS, H.	,,	18–11–17
Gnr.	HUNT, J.	,,	18–11–17
Gnr.	KIRKHOPE, J.	,,	18–11–17
Bdr.	COWLEY, W. F.	,,	20–11–17
Gnr.	McNICHOL, M.	,,	20–11–17
Gnr.	McMILLAN, D.	,,	18–11–17
Corpl.	CROSS, F.	,,	19–11–17
Sergt.	BILTON, J.	Wounded (Gas)	19–11–17
Corpl.	HICKS, A. E.	,,	19–11–17
Bdr.	GUMMER, H. A.	,,	19–11–17
Bdr.	NICHOLSON, A. J.	,,	19–11–17
Bdr.	REGAN, J.	,,	19–11–17
A/Corpl.	PRITCHARD, P.	,,	19–11–17
Sergt.	SMITH, P.	,,	19–11–17
Gnr.	MARTIN, A. S.	,,	19–11–17
Gnr.	HARRISON, W.	,,	19–11–17
Gnr.	GRIMMETT, A. F.	,,	19–11–17
Sergt.	DIXON, A. C.	,,	19–11–17
Gnr.	CHAPMAN, G.	,,	19–11–17
Gnr.	SMITH, A. C.	,,	19–11–17
Gnr.	RUMBLES, A. J.	,,	19–11–17
Sergt.	LOVERY, W.	,,	19–11–17
Gnr.	KNOTT, C.	,,	19–11–17
Corpl.	WARD, R.	,,	19–11–17
Gnr.	COULSON, D. T.	,,	19–11–17
A/Bdr.	PAYNE, W. R.	,,	19–11–17
Gnr.	FROGGETT, E.	,,	19–11–17
Gnr.	McEWAN, J. B.	,,	19–11–17
Dvr.	McCREADIE, J.	,,	19–11–17
Corpl.	WILLIAMS, G.	,,	19–11–17
L/Bdr.	WALKER, P.	,,	19–11–17
L/Bdr.	COCKELL, E. J. H.	,,	19–11–17
Gnr.	BISHOP, W. H.	,,	24–11–17
Gnr.	MITCHELL, H.	,,	24–11–17
Gnr.	CRAWFORD, H. W.	,,	24–11–17
A/Bdr.	WRIGHT, R.	,,	24–11–17
Ftr/Cpl.	HOLDSWORTH, A.	,,	24–11–17
Gnr.	EDWARDS, A. V.	,,	24–11–17

RANK.	NAME.	NATURE OF CASUALTY.	DATE.
Gnr.	HARRAWAY, A. E.	Wounded (Gas)	24–11–17
Gnr.	NEWTON, W.	,,	24–11–17
Gnr.	EVANS, G. H.	Wounded	19–11–17
Gnr.	DONAGHUE, J.	Died	7–12–17
Bdr.	TERRY, E.	Died of wounds	3–12–17
Gnr.	WOOD, A.	Killed in action	5–12–17
Gnr.	LOVETT, J. B.	,,	5–12–17
Gnr.	EDMONDS, H. E.	,,	5–12–17
Gnr.	LOCK, J. G.	,,	5–12–17
Dvr.	STIMPSON, C. R.	Wounded	19–11–17
Gnr.	CRAWFORD, H. W.	,,	24–11–17
Gnr.	MITCHELL, H.	,,	24–11–17
Gnr.	BISHOP, W. H.	,,	24–11–17
Gnr.	VEASEY, F. J.	,,	5–12–17
Corpl.	EDE, A.	,,	5–12–17
Dvr.	WALSH, F.	,,	5–12–17
Dvr.	EDGELEY, E.	,,	5–12–17
Dvr.	ROBSON, A.	,,	5–12–17
Dvr.	RUMENS, C. W.	,,	5–12–17
Gnr.	RHYMES, W. H.	,,	5–12–17
Gnr.	BURFOOT, E. S.	Died of wounds	15–12–17
Bdr.	MONKS, E.	Wounded	9–12–17
Sergt.	PITT, C. E.	,,	9–12–17
Gnr.	HARRISON, G. H.	,,	14–12–17
Gnr.	CHANT, J.	,,	14–12–17
Gnr.	LLOYD, J.	,,	13–12–17
Gnr.	SMITH, J.	,,	13–12–17
Gnr.	BURDEN, S. B.	,,	13–12–17
Whlr/Cpl.	MILES, J. W.	,,	13–12–17
Gnr.	HARRINGTON, F. A.	Died of wounds	31–12–17
Gnr.	DANBY, J. W.	Wounded	11–12–17
Corpl.	HART, C. H.	,,	11–12–17
A/Corpl.	HANCOCK, F.	,,	10–12–17
Gnr.	PIKE, E. A.	,,	14–12–17
Corpl.	HART, W. R.	Killed in action	11–12–17
L/Bdr.	MURBY, E. S.	,,	12–12–17
Gnr.	SMITH, P.	Wounded	14–12–17
Gnr.	WEBB, W. J.	,,	18–12–17
Dvr.	SMITH, W. L.	,,	12–12–17
S/S.	STACEY, A. H.	,,	22–12–17
L/Bdr.	MARTIN, T.	,,	22–12–17
Dvr.	BUAS, A. B.	,,	22–12–17
Gnr.	ROBINSON, C.	,,	22–12–17
Gnr.	INCE, H.	,,	3–12–17
Bdr.	STILL, A. J.	,,	3–12–17
Dvr.	PARKER, J.	Killed in action	31–12–17
Gnr.	O'BRIEN, J.	Died of wounds	12– 1–18
Dvr.	EARLY, J.	Wounded	11– 1–18
Gnr.	WILLIAMS, T. H.	,,	11– 1–18
Gnr.	MITCHELL, L.	,,	11– 1–18
Gnr.	OGILVIE, D. R.	,,	11– 1–18
Dvr.	WYATT, S. E.	,,	3–12–17
L/Bdr.	HAYES, W. J.	,,	11– 1–18
Sergt.	LOWERY, W.	,,	10– 1–18

RANK.	NAME.	NATURE OF CASUALTY.	DATE.
Dvr.	JOHNSON, S. M.	Killed in action	11– 1–18
Gnr.	BROWN, E.	,,	11– 1–18
A/Corpl.	COLLINS, J.	Wounded	10– 3–18
Sergt.	MANSELL, A.	,,	23– 3–18
Fitter	BAMFORD, P.	,,	26– 3–18
Gnr.	RAY, A.	,,	3– 4–18
Gnr.	WRIGHT, F. C.	,,	29– 3–18
Gnr.	ROUD, T.	,,	22– 3–18
Gnr.	BADGER, B.	,,	26– 3–18
Gnr.	HODGKINS, E.	,,	26– 3–18
L/Bdr.	LEA, W.	,,	30– 3–18
Gnr.	TRUNKFIELD, G.	,,	30– 3–18
Dvr.	DELL, G.	,,	31– 3–18
B.S.M.	PYPER, A.	,,	30– 3–18
Dvr.	LOTT, H. C.	,,	29– 3–18
Gnr.	SHUTT, V.	,,	30– 3–18
Dvr.	GAMBLE, J. W.	,,	4– 4–18
Sergt.	ALCOCK, C. D.	,,	4– 4–18
Dvr.	WATSON, C.	,,	4– 4–18
Dvr.	COLSTON, J. R.	,,	4– 4–18
Dvr.	DIXON, T.	,,	4– 4–18
Gnr.	SHACKLETON, H.	,,	4– 4–18
Sergt.	MARSHALL, R. J.	Killed in action	24– 3–18
Fitter	BAMFORD, P.	Died of wounds	26– 3–18
Gnr.	DAVIES, W.	,,	28– 3–18
Dvr.	WOODMAN, J.	Wounded	25– 3–18
Gnr.	HORN, W. R.	,,	25– 3–18
L/Bdr.	CHENERY, W. T.	,,	25– 3–18
Gnr.	DAW, G. H.	,,	24– 3–18
Dvr.	MATTHEWMAN, G. R.	,,	4– 4–18
Dvr.	SEAGRAVE, P.	,,	27– 3–18
Dvr.	COX, P. J.	,,	24– 3–18
Sergt.	BILTON, J.	,,	27– 3–18
Dvr.	KERR, J.	,,	4– 4–18
Gnr.	SALT, J.	,,	4– 4–18
Gnr.	WALSH, H.	,,	4– 4–18
Corpl.	LAWSON, A. W.	,,	4– 4–18
Gnr.	ADLAM, G.	,,	6– 4–18
Gnr.	SHADDOCK, M.	,,	6– 4–18
Dvr.	CHANDLER, W. F.	,,	29– 3–18
Gnr.	CLARK, E.	,,	29– 3–18
Dvr.	CROSS, A.	,,	30– 3–18
Sergt.	PEACOCK, D.	,,	23– 3–18
Dvr.	FLETCHER, L.	,,	29– 3–18
Gnr.	HARRIS, D. L.	,,	2– 4–18
Gnr.	LOWE, F. C.	,,	4– 4–18
Sergt.	ROBINSON, W. M.	,,	31– 3–18
Gnr.	CUMPSTEY, E.	,,	1– 4–18
Dvr.	GWILLIAM, E. W.	Killed in action	28– 3–18
Dvr.	PRESHO, G.	,,	4– 4–18
Dvr.	EBDEN, J. H. W.	,,	4– 4–18
Dvr.	WEEKS, A. L.	,,	4– 4–18
Gnr.	MOORE, F.	,,	4– 4–18
Dvr.	BARNARD, C.	,,	4– 4–18

RANK.	NAME.	NATURE OF CASUALTY.	DATE.
Dvr.	BOND, S. P.	Killed in action	28– 3–18
Bdr.	McGREGOR, T.	,,	9– 4–18
Dvr.	RISI, B.	,,	9– 4–18
Dvr.	WEST, W. J.	,,	10– 4–18
Gnr.	WHITTINGTON, W.	,,	6– 4–18
Gnr.	AIRD, J.	,,	9– 4–18
Gnr.	RAY, A.	,,	6– 4–18
Dvr.	REDDINGTON, N.	Died of wounds	6– 4–18
Gnr.	HACKETT, W. A.	,,	10– 4–18
Dvr.	BANFILL, H. J.	,,	12– 4–18
Gnr.	TAYLOR, J. S.	,,	9– 4–18
Gnr.	ALLAN, C.	Wounded	29– 3–18
Dvr.	MOORE, W. J.	,,	31– 3–18
L/Bdr.	TOOLILL, T.	,,	4– 4–18
Gnr.	CORFIELD, J. C.	,,	4– 4–18
Dvr.	FRYER, C. W.	,,	9– 4–18
Gnr.	DISHART, A. D.	,,	8– 4–18
Gnr.	KEYLOCK, W. J.	,,	8– 4–18
Dvr.	TAYLOR, H.	,,	10– 4–18
Corpl.	BRANCH, G. W.	,,	4– 4–18
Gnr.	STRAUGHAN, G. N.	,,	4– 4–18
Gnr.	NORTON, P. E.	,,	4– 4–18
Gnr.	CARRIGAN, G.	,,	12– 4–18
L/Bdr.	RYLAND, W.	,,	12– 4–18
Gnr.	HEDGES, P.	,,	9– 4–18
Gnr.	ENGLAND, F.	,,	12– 4–18
Gnr.	WICKHAM, R. R.	,,	12– 4–18
Dvr.	BAIRD, A. J. F.	,,	12– 4–18
Gnr.	CONLEY, C. J.	,,	30– 3–18
Dvr.	CAVE, A. J.	,,	6– 4–18
Dvr.	ROBERTSON, A.	,,	6– 4–18
Bdr.	FREEMAN, W. L.	,,	4– 4–18
Gnr.	GOODING, R.	,,	12– 4–18
Gnr.	HOWARD, A.	,,	12– 4–18
Dvr.	BRYAN, W. W.	,,	9– 4–18
Bdr.	ALLEN, W.	,,	10– 4–18
Dvr.	JAMES, H. W.	,,	30– 3–19
Bdr.	McGILLIVRAY, A.	,,	7– 4–18
Dvr.	JONES, J.	,,	4– 4–18
Fitter	HALL, R. H.	,,	5– 4–18
L/Bdr.	McCLUGHAN, G. W.	,,	8– 4–18
A/Sergt.	BRENCHLEY, S. D.	,,	29– 3–18
Dvr.	RICHARDSON, F. G.	,,	30– 3–18
Gnr.	ALLCOCK, J. S.	,,	9– 4–18
A/Corpl.	WALKER, E. J.	,,	7– 4–18
Gnr.	KIRKPATRICK, S.	,,	7– 4–18
Dvr.	SIMPKIN, F.	,,	7– 4–18
Dvr.	WOODFORD, F. C.	,,	7– 4–18
Dvr.	McDADE, H.	,,	7– 4–18
A/Bdr.	PRATT, H.	,,	13– 4–18
Dvr.	HEWITT, H. W.	,,	9– 4–18
L/Bdr.	ARCHER, W.	,,	8– 4–18
Gnr.	SHADDOCK, M.	,,	8– 4–18
Sergt.	STRACHAN, J.	,,	8– 4–18

RANK.	NAME.	NATURE OF CASUALTY.	DATE.
Gnr.	WELLS, A. G.	Wounded	9- 4-18
Gnr.	STUBBS, L.	,, (Accidental)	11- 2-18
Dvr.	VALLER, G. J.	,,	23- 3-18
L/Bdr.	CAREY, R. G.	,,	6- 4-18
Gnr.	DRAYTON, W. J.	,,	9- 4-18
A/Sergt.	DONALDSON, A. A.	,,	10- 4-18
Dvr.	SLADE, J.	,,	9- 4-18
Bdr.	TURTON, A.	Killed in action	6- 4-18
Gnr.	HARRIS, D.	Died of wounds	3- 4-18
Dvr.	BROWN, H.	Wounded	4- 4-18
Dvr.	CRAIG, R.	,,	4- 4-18
Dvr.	DE-LA-BARRE, A.	,,	11- 4-18
Dvr.	PRESLAND, J.	,,	4- 4-18
Gnr.	WRIGHT, C. F.	Died of wounds	5- 4-18
Gnr.	BARKER, C.	Wounded	15- 4-18
Gnr.	DRAYTON, W. J.	,,	10- 4-18
Gnr.	DAVIES, J.	,,	13- 4-18
Bdr.	KIPLING, W.	,, (Accidental)	19- 4-18
Gnr.	BRACKENBOROUGH, L.G.A	Killed in action	11- 4-18
Gnr.	PAYNE, T.	Wounded	6- 5-18
Sergt.	HEY, W. H.	,,	9- 5-18
Gnr.	SMITH, T. M.	,,	17- 5-18
Dvr.	RANKIN, J.	,,	21- 5-18
Dvr.	FOURACRE, J.	,,	21- 5-18
Gnr.	KNIGHT, W. J.	,,	21- 5-18
Bdr.	SPACEY, S. H.	,,	25- 5-18
Gnr.	MUMFORD, F. C.	,,	25- 5-18
Gnr.	ISHERWOOD, W.	Died of wounds	2- 6-18
Gnr.	MUNDY, R.	,,	6- 6-18
Sergt.	FLINT, A. J.	,,	5- 6-18
L/Bdr.	WHITE, A. R.	Wounded	29- 5-18
A/Sergt.	DONALDSON, A. A.	,,	3- 6-18
Gnr.	SIMPSON, G.	,,	3- 6-18
Gnr.	McLUGHAN, G.	Died of wounds	11- 6-18
L/Bdr.	AYRES, F.	Wounded (Gas)	2- 6-18
A/Corpl.	COLLINS, J.	,,	2- 6-18
Bdr.	WARD, G.	,,	2- 6-18
A/Bdr.	SKINNER, E.	,,	2- 6-18
Fitter	BOAST, J.	,,	2- 6-18
A/Sergt.	WILLIAMS, W. A.	,,	2- 6-18
Gnr.	BENTLEY, E.	,,	2- 6-18
Gnr.	YATES, F. S.	,,	2- 6-18
A/Corpl.	SAGGERS, C. W.	,,	2- 6-18
Sergt.	EDKINS, J. C.	,,	2- 6-18
Gnr.	ROBSON, R. A.	,,	2- 6-18
Gnr.	GRACE, M. J.	,,	2- 6-18
Gnr.	JONES, F. C.	,,	2- 6-18
Gnr.	O'NEIL, H.	,,	2- 6-18
Gnr.	COOMBES, J.	,,	2- 6-18
L/Bdr.	WINN, W. H.	,,	2- 6-18
Gnr.	HALLWOOD, J.	,,	2- 6-18
Gnr.	PACKHAM, F.	,,	5- 6-18
Bdr.	BALSDON, C.	,,	5- 6-18
L/Bdr.	GOLDACRE, W. C.	Wounded	22- 5-18

Appendix " D "—*contd.*

RANK.	NAME.	NATURE OF CASUALTY.	DATE.
Corpl.	May, H.	Wounded	4– 6–18
Gnr.	Masson, A.	,,	6– 6–18
Bdr.	Crawshay, H. C.	,,	7– 6–18
Gnr.	Hopkins, J. W. H.	,,	7– 6–18
Gnr.	Proud, J. E.	,,	7– 6–18
Gnr.	Taylor, W.	,,	7– 6–18
Gnr.	Lynch, W.	,,	7– 6–18
Gnr.	Allen, L. M.	,,	3– 6–18
Bdr.	Durkin, T.	,,	9– 6–18
Gnr.	Stammers, P. E.	,,	8– 6–18
Gnr.	Duffield, B.	,,	10– 6–18
L/Bdr.	King, A.	,,	14– 6–18
Dvr.	Jowett, E.	,,	14– 6–18
Corpl.	Beach, B.	,,	16– 6–18
Gnr.	Mount, C. A.	,,	16– 6–18
L/Bdr.	Gibbons, F.	,,	17– 6–18
Sergt.	Laskey, H. S.	,,	2– 6–18
Gnr.	Smith, W.	,,	15– 6–18
Gnr.	Beardmore, W. E. L.	,,	11– 7–18
Dvr.	Hurdle, J.	Wounded and missing	24– 3–18
Dvr.	Parsons, H. M. J.	Killed in action	16– 7–18
Gnr.	Devaney, F.	Wounded	16– 7–18
Dvr.	Batey, C.	,,	17– 7–18
Gnr.	Mullins, F. E.	,,	18– 7–18
Dvr.	Mackintosh, C. J.	,,	17– 7–18
Dvr.	Crout, T. W.	,,	26– 7–18
Bdr.	Capeling, A. E.	,,	26– 7–18
Gnr.	Thompson, J.	Died of wounds	26– 7–18
Gnr.	Hinks, F.	Wounded	26– 7–18
Dvr.	Boyles, W.	,,	25– 7–18
Gnr.	Greaves, J. E.	,,	12– 8–18
Gnr.	Elvin, A.	,,	20– 8–18
Sergt.	Seabrook, H. G.	,,	21– 8–18
Corpl.	Buckle, C. A.	,,	21– 8–18
Gnr.	Harrison, G. W.	,,	13– 8–18
Gnr.	Simpson, G. F.	,,	24– 8–18
Corpl.	Mitchell, R.	,,	24– 8–18
Gnr.	Buckland, S. A.	,,	24– 8–18
Bdr.	Child, S. A.	,,	24– 8–18
Gnr.	Nicholson, G. E.	Died of wounds	31– 8–18
Gnr.	Pearson, H.	,,	31– 8–18
Gnr.	Lenham, A. J.	Killed in action	30– 8–18
Gnr.	Stevens, J. E.	Died of wounds	3– 9–18
Bdr.	Smith, A. E.	,,	2– 9–18
Gnr.	Bloxson, F.	,,	3– 9–18
Dvr.	Price, J.	Wounded	24– 8–18
Dvr.	Fitzgerald, L. S.	,,	28– 8–18
L/Bdr.	Holland, A. H.	,,	1– 9–18
L/Bdr.	Procopides, E.	,,	1– 9–18
Dvr.	Amner, F.	Killed in action	2– 9–18
Dvr.	Boynes, W.	,,	30– 8–18
Dvr.	Harrison, H.	,,	31– 8–18
Gnr.	Sheaf, F. R.	,,	2– 9–18
Dvr.	Twine, J. H.	,,	2– 9–18

RANK.	NAME.	NATURE OF CASUALTY.	DATE.
Gnr.	Smith, T.	Died of wounds	13– 9–18
Gnr.	Dawson, T.	,,	14– 9–18
Gnr.	Vine, R. H.	Killed in action	9– 9–18
Sergt.	Kille, H. B.	Wounded	30– 8–18
Sergt.	Pitt, C. E.	,,	30– 8–18
Dvr.	Grogan, W.	,,	30– 8–18
Dvr.	Branch, C. F.	,,	30– 8–18
Gnr.	Garner, F.	,,	30– 8–18
Dvr.	Webb, M.	,,	30– 8–18
Gnr.	Norman, H. S.	,,	30– 8–18
Dvr.	Ansell, G. H.	,,	31– 8–18
Gnr.	Luck, F.	,,	29– 8–18
Dvr.	Stanton, J.	,,	27– 8–18
Gnr.	Reynolds, A.	,,	31– 8–18
Gnr.	Abbott, W. H.	,,	31– 8–18
Gnr.	Connelly, A.	,,	1– 9–18
Gnr.	Pierce, H. A.	,,	1– 9–18
Fitter	Jager, J.	,,	7– 9–18
Gnr.	Sellers, R.	,,	7– 9–18
Gnr.	Wren, J.	,,	7– 9–18
Gnr.	Waller, S. W. J.	,,	7– 9–18
Gnr.	Petty, R. F.	,,	7– 9–18
Gnr.	Lloyd. F.	,,	7– 9–18
Gnr.	Mount, C. A.	,,	7– 9–18
Gnr.	Boyle, J.	,,	7– 9–18
Dvr.	O'Neill, P.	,,	7– 9–18
Gnr.	Jamieson, J.	,,	7– 9–18
L/Bdr.	Nash, A. W.	,,	27– 8–18
Sergt.	Fray, D.	,,	1– 9–18
Gnr.	Moon, H. F.	,,	2– 9–18
Dvr.	Mooney, W.	,,	1– 9–18
Dvr.	Davies, W.	,,	7– 9–18
Gnr.	Nash, J. W.	,,	7– 9–18
Gnr.	Spencer, J.	,,	7– 9–18
Gnr.	Mudd, W.	,,	7– 9–18
Dvr.	Smith, H. W.	,,	3– 9–18
Dvr.	Pope, H.	,,	1– 9–18
Gnr.	Sivier, G.	,,	2– 9–18
Sergt.	Ajax, E.	,,	3– 9–18
Gnr.	Mell, A. T.	,,	2– 9–18
Gnr.	Parker, G.	,,	8– 9–18
Sergt.	Jellyman, J.	,,	9– 9–18
Gnr.	Gibson, R. W.	Died of wounds	17– 9–18
Gnr.	Bowen, A. W.	,,	29– 8–18
Dvr.	Rooney, J.	Wounded	27– 8–18
Sergt.	Hird, J.	,,	7– 9–18
Dvr.	Lane, L.	,,	5– 9–18
Gnr.	Taylor, J. W.	,,	5– 9–18
Gnr.	Griffin, J.	,,	2– 9–18
Gnr.	Whittaker, S.	,,	7– 9–18
Gnr.	Rishton, H.	,,	8– 9–18
Bde.	Burgess, C.	,,	8– 9–18
Corpl.	Arnold, E. W.	,,	8– 9–18
L/Bdr.	Boyce, T. W.	,,	8– 9–18

RANK.	NAME.	NATURE OF CASUALTY.	DATE.
Gnr.	BADGER, B.	Wounded	8– 9–18
Dvr.	COBB, C. F.	,,	9– 9–18
Dvr.	AUSTIN, C. J.	,,	9– 9–18
Gnr.	ALLISON, A. J.	,,	9– 9–18
Gnr.	KRAMPE, J.	,,	9– 9–18
Gnr.	SHARPER, W.	,,	9– 9–18
Gnr.	TOWELL, W.	,,	13– 9–18
Gnr.	CUNDALL, W. T.	,,	14– 9–18
Gnr.	NOCKS, T. E.	,,	13– 9–18
Gnr.	SARGENT, C.	,,	13– 8–18
Corpl.	AVERY, T.	,,	14– 9–18
L/Bdr.	MOORE, W. G.	,,	14– 9–18
Dvr.	LOFTHOUSE, F. H.	,,	11– 9–18
Gnr.	DINSDALE, J. M.	,,	11– 9–18
Dvr.	CANNON, G.	,,	2– 9–18
Gnr.	GOODMAN, H. J.	,,	7– 9–18
Gnr.	DENNISON, G. H.	,,	8– 9–18
Dvr.	BUTLER, A.	,,	8– 9–18
Gnr.	WISE, W. J.	,,	8– 9–18
Gnr.	REEDER, T.	,,	7– 9–18
Gnr.	HARRISON, R. P.	,,	19– 9–18
Dvr.	GREEN, A. L.	,,	13– 9–18
Dvr.	VALLER, G. J.	,,	8– 9–18
Gnr.	McINTYRE, W.	,,	19– 8–18
Bdr.	WALTERS, E. A.	,,	16– 9–18
Gnr.	BURGESS, G. S.	,,	21– 9–18
Sergt.	CANDLING, J. A.	Died of wounds	28– 9–18
Dvr.	BIBBY, T.	Killed in action	25– 9–18
Dvr.	BELCHER, H.	,,	25– 9–18
Dvr.	PEERS, J.	,,	26– 9–18
Gnr.	DODDS, E. P.	Died of wounds	28– 9–18
Sergt.	SCRIVEN, W.	,,	27– 9–18
Bdr.	VINING, S. A.	Wounded	22– 9–18
Gnr.	SCOTT, A. G.	,,	6– 9–18
Sergt.	CLAGGETT, J. W.	,,	24– 9–18
Sergt.	KNOX, W. R.	,,	23– 9–18
Corpl.	MITCHELL, R.	Wounded (remained at duty)	25– 9–18
L/Bdr.	MOON, F.	,,	25– 9–18
Gnr.	HAYTON, H.	,,	26– 9–18
Dvr.	ROBINSON, G.	Prisoner of war	15– 4–18
Dvr.	LYONS, W.	Died of wounds	2–10–18
Gnr.	NASH, J. W.	,,	3–10–18
Corpl.	TURNER, L.	,,	1–10–18
Dvr.	JONES, E. E.	Killed in action	28– 9–18
Dvr.	MACKLIN, P.	,,	28– 9–18
Dvr.	WEBB, M.	Died of wounds	5–10–18
Gnr.	ROBERTS, D. T.	Wounded	27– 9–18
Dvr.	ADDEYMAN, F.	,,	27– 9–18
Dvr.	THORNTON, F. C.	,,	29– 9–18
Gnr.	POOLE, J. J.	,,	29– 9–18
Dvr.	STUBBS, L.	,,	29– 9–18
Gnr.	SWEENEY, P.	,,	27– 9–18
Dvr.	BURTON, H. R.	,,	29– 9–18

RANK.	NAME.	NATURE OF CASUALTY.	DATE.
Dvr.	JACKSON, F.	Wounded	2–10–18
Gnr.	WILLIAMS, A. J.	,,	29– 9–18
Bdr.	VOSPER, A.	,,	27– 9–18
Gnr.	ALLISON, A. J.	,,	28– 9–18
Gnr.	SOMMERVILLE, F. J.	,,	1–10–18
Sergt.	HARRIS, G.	,,	28– 9–18
S/S.	IRELAND, J. H.	Killed in action	4–10–18
Gnr.	STEWART, A.	Died of wounds	14–10–18
Gnr.	McGILL, P.	Wounded	29– 9–18
Sergt.	McPHERSON, D.	,,	29– 9–18
Gnr.	MORAN, T.	,,	30– 9–18
Gnr.	BISHOP, E. G.	,,	1–10–18
Dvr.	WILLCOCKS, W.	,,	1–10–18
Gnr.	HUGHES, F.	,,	2–10–18
Gnr.	ROBERTS, W.	,,	13–10–18
L/Bdr.	GRAHAM, J.	,,	13–10–18
Gnr.	SIMBSON, F. J.	,,	13–10–18
Dvr.	HURDLE, J.	Prisoner of war	24– 3–18
Dvr.	MINNETT, W. A.	Died of wounds	14–10–18
Gnr.	KING, A.	Killed in action	13–10–18
L/Bdr.	SYKES, G.	,,	13–10–18
L/Bdr.	SMITH, W.	,,	13–10–18
Gnr.	THOMPSON, G.	,,	13–10–18
Bdr.	THORNE, F. C.	Wounded	27– 9–18
Gnr.	PETCHELL, J. P.	,,	13–10–18
Dvr.	ARMER, J. W.	,,	13–10–18
Gnr.	STOWELL, J. W.	,,	13–10–18
L/Bdr.	WHITE, A. R.	,,	13–10–18
Gnr.	McHUGH, J.	,,	13–10–18
Corpl.	DRISCOLL, M.	,,	13–10–18
Bdr.	HOSKINS, J.	,,	13–10–18
Dvr.	EAST, J.	,,	13–10–18
Gnr.	POWELL, T.	,,	14–10–18
Bdr.	DREW, G. W.	,,	14–10–18
A/Sergt.	GUMMER, H. J. A.	,,	13–10–18
Corpl.	JACQUES, E.	,,	13–10–18
Dvr.	LOGAN, J.	,,	13–10–18
Bdr.	TYE, J. E.	,,	13–10–18
Dvr.	FOLEY, C.	,,	14–10–18
L/Bdr.	SIMPKIN, F.	,,	14–10–18
Dvr.	DOBSON, J.	,,	14–10–18
Gnr.	WRIGHT, W. C.	,,	13–10–18
Fitter	YAYLOR, D. A.	,,	24–10–18
L/Bdr.	WALLBANK, H. S.	,,	19–10–18
Gnr.	ALLEN, R.	,,	19–10–18
Gnr.	DOPSON, P. A.	,,	19–10–18
Siglr.	BOWES, R.	Killed in action	25–10–18
Sergt.	MEHAFFEY. R.	Wounded	26– 9–18
Dvr.	RUTTERFORD, H.	,,	13–10–18
Gnr.	YOUNG, W.	,,	13–10–18
Gnr.	SHORE, A.	,,	15–10–18
Dvr.	CHADWICK, J. T.	,,	23–10–18
Gnr.	BEIGHTON, H.	,,	20–10–18
Dvr.	WALKER, A. E.	,,	24–10–18

RANK.	NAME.	NATURE OF CASUALTY.	DATE.
Corpl.	AVERY, T.	Died of wounds	8–11–18
Gnr.	ABBOTT, W. H.	Died (Pneumonia)	3–11–18
Dvr.	MUSGRAVE, D.	,,	8–11–18
Gnr.	HIRST, L. N.	Wounded	27–10–18
Gnr.	KEENAN, J.	,,	27–10–18
Gnr.	WALKER, J.	,,	25–10–18
Gnr.	RYAN, T.	,,	27–10–18
Gnr.	WATSON, D.	,,	27–10–18
Gnr.	BROWN, G.	,,	28–10–18
Ftr/S/Sgt.	BABER, G.	,,	30–10–18
Corpl.	MILLS, W.	,,	30–10–18
Gnr.	FAIRWEATHER, W.	,,	31–10–18
Gnr.	SHARPER, W.	,,	31–10–18
Sergt.	SANDS, W. A.	,,	31–10–18
Gnr.	GARNER, F.	,,	29–10–18
Siglr.	GREENMAN, T.	,,	29–10–18
Siglr.	STEWART, C.	,,	31–10–18
Gnr.	ALLMOOD, S.	,,	1–11–18
Gnr.	NEVILLE, G.	,,	1–11–18
Corpl.	PAINTER, H. G.	Died (Pneumonia)	22–11–18
Sadd/Sgt.	GAWN, C. W.	,,	23–11–18
Sergt.	BAKER, A. G.	Wounded	30–10–18
Gnr.	GURNEY, J. R.	Died (Appendicitis)	3–12–18

184th Brigade, R.F.A.

RANK.	NAME.	NATURE OF CASUALTY.	DATE.
Gnr.	TAYLOR, W.	Wounded	26– 4–16
Gnr.	TAYLOR, W.	,,	20– 6–16
Sergt.	IFOULD, F.	,,	13– 7–16
Gnr.	FLEMING, J. W.	,,	1– 7–16
Gnr.	NOBLE, A.	,,	13– 7–16
Gnr.	BRIGGS, J. W.	,,	21– 7–16
Corpl.	WEBB, J. A.	,,	27– 7–16
Sergt.	BOLTON, A.	,,	29– 7–16
Gnr.	THOMPSON, J.	,,	7– 8–16
Dvr.	EADES, A. J.	Died of wounds	3– 9–16
Gnr.	ROSSITER, F.	Wounded	3– 9–16
Dvr.	TUDMAN, W. J.	,,	11– 9–16
Dvr.	TAYLOR, R. W.	,,	18– 9–16
Gnr.	HAYWOOD, W.	Died of wounds	6–10–16
Gnr.	BROOKS, V.	Wounded	6–10–16
Dvr.	NEALE, T.	,,	7–10–16
Gnr.	REILLY, T.	,,	6–10–16
Dvr.	ARNOLD, J. H.	Killed in action	13–11–16
Corpl.	HOMER, S. M.	,,	13–11–16

184th Brigade, R.F.A., was disbanded 1–12–1916, on re-organisation of 39th Divisional Artillery.

39th Div. Ammunition Column.

RANK.	NAME.	NATURE OF CASUALTY.	DATE.
Gnr.	McGILLAN, R.	Wounded	16– 7–16
Gnr.	HANLEY, J. J.	Died of wounds	18– 7–16
Dvr.	KEEP, J.	,,	18– 7–16
Gnr.	COMMONS, T. H.	Wounded	18– 7–16
Dvr.	JAKES, B. A.	,,	18– 7–16
Gnr.	MARTIN, T. H.	,,	19– 7–16
Dvr.	PRICE, J.	,,	6– 8–16
Dvr.	PRICE, J.	,,	6– 9–16
Gnr.	JARVIS, A. F.	Died of wounds	14– 9–16
Gnr.	DUCKWORTH, B.	Wounded	28– 9–16
Dvr.	NICHOLLS, W.	,,	28– 9–16
Gnr.	ROYLE, T.	,,	28– 9–16
Bdr.	JOHNSTON, W. F., R.G.A.	,,	1–10–16
Gnr.	ROWLANDS, G. R.	,,	30– 9–16
Gnr.	WILBOURNE, G. R.	,,	29– 9–16
A/Bdr.	THOMPSON, A.	,,	11–10–16
Gnr.	WILDS, A.	Killed in action	Not kn.
Gnr.	TIBBITS, A. O.	Wounded	8–11–16
A/Sergt.	BLACKLEDGE, R. J.	Died	21–11–16
Dvr.	BROWN, R. J. L.	,,	12–12–16
Gnr.	SCOTT, J.	Wounded	8– 1–17
Dvr.	BARRETT, A. H.	,,	9– 2–17
Dvr.	WINTERBOTTOM, C.	Killed in action	6– 6–17
Dvr.	ROBB, J.	,,	6– 6–17
Dvr.	ELLIOTT, A. J.	,,	6– 6–17
S/Smith	HALLEY, W.	Wounded	6– 6–17
Gnr.	HARRISON, L.	,,	6– 6–17
Dvr.	RICHARDSON, W. H.	,,	7– 6–17
Gnr.	WISE, R. W.	,,	7– 6–17
Dvr.	ROWLAND, S. C.	,,	6– 6–17
Dvr.	BRANEY, J. T.	,,	15 6–17
Dvr.	SAUNDERS, A.	,,	15 6–17
Dvr.	KEEBLE, W.	,,	20 6–17
Dvr.	RICH, A. W. C.	Killed in action	26 6–17
Gnr.	FIVEASH, G. W.	,,	5– 7–17
Dvr.	RICKETTS, S. S.	,,	5– 7–17
S/Smith	GROVES, J.	Wounded	25– 6–17
Dvr.	HYLAND, C. F.	,,	5– 7–17
Dvr.	THISTLETHWAITE, W.	,,	25– 6–17
Dvr.	WHITTAKER, H.	,,	25– 6–17
Gnr.	GARLICK, W. T.	,,	5– 7–17
Sergt.	NEWTON, J.	,,	5– 7–17
Gnr.	WOOD, R.	,,	5– 7–17
Dvr.	PARSONS, W.	,,	5– 7–17
Dvr.	KEEPS, F. G.	,,	5– 7–17
Farr/Sgt.	WELLMAN, C.	,,	5– 7–17
Gnr.	SMITH, J.	,,	21– 6–17
Dvr.	OWENS, G.	,,	21– 6–17
Bdr.	ABBS, C. F.	,,	25– 6–17
Dvr.	CHAMPION, E. E.	,,	25– 6–17
Dvr.	OWEN, W. H.	,,	14– 7–17
Gnr.	OWEN, A.	,,	5– 7–17
Gnr.	VOLKERT, J.	,,	5– 7–17

Appendix " D "—contd.

RANK.	NAME.	NATURE OF CASUALTY.	DATE.
Dvr.	GROGAN, T.	Wounded	25– 6–17
Gnr.	CREEVY, J.	,,	25– 7–17
Gnr.	FORD, R.	,,	25– 7–17
Gnr.	WHITING, F.	,,	31– 7–17
Gnr.	SMALL, W.	,,	25– 7–17
Dvr.	BARNSDALE, C. F.	,,	3– 8–17
Dvr.	CONNOR, P.	,,	8– 7–17
Gnr.	MITCHELL, R. C. R.	,,	5– 8–17
Dvr.	WEAVER, E. G.	,,	8– 7–17
Dvr.	AINSWORTH, W.	,,	5– 8–17
Saddler	WOODHOUSE, F.	,,	5– 8–17
S/S.	BLAIN, H.	Killed in action	5– 8–17
Dvr.	PERRY, S.	,,	5– 8–17
Dvr.	DEVENISH, H.	,,	7– 8–17
Gnr.	ROLLINSON, H.	Died of wounds	12– 8–17
Gnr.	TYLER, H. M.	,,	12– 8–17
Dvr.	DIXON, W. C.	Wounded	12– 8–17
Gnr.	FAULKNER, E.	,,	12– 8–17
Dvr.	GROGAN, T.	,,	8– 8–17
Dvr.	GREEN, F.	,,	12– 8–17
Dvr.	HAMILTON, F.	,,	5– 8–17
Dvr.	PASFIELD, R.	,,	12– 8–17
Dvr.	SMITH, A. S.	,,	12– 8–17
Wheeler	CARVER, J. R.	,,	5– 8–17
Gnr.	BEASLEY, G.	,,	12– 8–17
Dvr.	PITHERS, R.	,,	25– 6–17
Gnr.	TARRANT, C. W.	,,	12– 8–17
Dvr.	WATSON, H.	,,	14– 8–17
Gnr.	HONNAN, W.	,,	14– 8–17
Farr-Sgt.	BLAKE, F.	,,	19– 8–17
Dvr.	COLEMAN, H. A.	,,	25– 9–17
Gnr.	McCLARNON, W.	,,	14– 7–17
Bdr.	BELLAMY, J. G.	,,	16– 2–18
Gnr.	MARTYN, A.	,,	16– 2–18
Corpl.	FARMER, D. W.	Died (Lobar pneu.)	14–11–17
Gnr.(L/Bdr.)	WINTERBOTTOM, J.	Killed in action	16– 2–18
Dvr.	JONES, W.	,,	16– 2–17
Gnr.	MAJOR, G.	,,	16– 2–18
Gnr.	DODD, W.	,,	23– 2–18
Gnr.	MOULE, H.	Wounded	16– 2–18
Gnr.	MUNROE, G. B.	,,	16– 2–18
Gnr.	TUNESI, A.	,,	16– 2–18
Gnr.	CHRISTIE, A.	,,	23– 2–18
Gnr.	CORNEY, W. J. P.	,,	24– 2–18
S/S.	BAILEY, W. G.	,,	9– 3–18
S/S.	ALLSOPP, G.	Killed in action	9– 3–18
Dvr.	CONNELL, W.	Wounded	25– 3–18
Bdr.	COLLINS, T. E.	,,	5– 4–18
Dvr.	ROUTLEDGE, T.	,,	29– 3–18
Dvr.	KIMBLE, W. S.	Died of wounds	12– 4–18
Dvr.	AITKIN, G. S.	Wounded	12– 4–18
Gnr.	EWENS, J. H.	,,	12– 4–18
Corpl.	HOLDEN, A. H., M.M.	,,	6– 4–18
Dvr.	ROBERTS, G. F.	,,	12– 4–18

72

RANK.		NAME.			NATURE OF CASUALTY.	DATE.
Dvr.	..	ROULLIER, W.	..	..	Wounded	12– 4–18
Gnr.	..	TERRY, C.	..	..	,, ...	12– 4–18
Dvr.	..	BLISS, T. N.	..	..	Killed in action ..	12– 4–18
Dvr.	..	BRENNAN, E	..	..	,, ..	12–14–18
Dvr.	..	PENALIGON, W. J.	..	..	,, ...	12– 4–18
Dvr.	..	PRINCE, W.	..	..	Wounded	15– 4–18
Corpl.	..	CRUICKSHANKS, R.	..	..	,, ...	17– 5–18
Gnr.	..	ECCLES, G.	..	..	Killed in action ..	30– 5–18
Gnr.	..	GILLIARD, J.	..	..	Wounded (remained at duty)	30– 5–18
Gnr.	..	BENSON, J. P.	..	..	Wounded	29– 8–18
Dvr.	..	BULLOCK, C.	..	..	,, ..	26– 8–18
Dvr.	..	LOCKYER, A. V.	..	..	,, ..	29– 8–18
Dvr.	..	ROBERTS, J.	..	..	,, ..	29– 8–18
Dvr.	..	RAWLINS, J.	..	..	,, ..	29– 8–18
Dvr.	..	SHEARS, A. J.	..	..	,, ..	29– 8–18
Dvr.	..	YOUNG, S. E.	..	..	,, ..	29– 8–18
Saddler	..	JACEY, W.	..	..	Slightly wounded (remained at duty)	29– 8–18
Dvr.	..	MARTIN, L.	..	..	,, ,, ..	29– 8–18
Dvr.	..	PRATT, T.	..	..	,, ,,	29– 8–18
Gnr.	..	SHARROCKS, R. E.	..	..	,, ,, ..	29– 8–18
Gnr.	..	STAPLES, A.	..	..	,, ,, ..	29– 8–18
Dvr.	..	SULLIVAN, J. H.	..	..	,, ,, ..	29– 8–18
Gnr.	..	BEENHAM, J.	..	..	Died of wounds ..	3– 9–18
Bdr.	..	CHILMAN, A. W.	..	..	Wounded ..	31– 8–18
Gnr.	..	REARMAIN, A.	..	..	,,	6– 9–18
Dvr.	..	RICHARDSON, W. J.	..	..	,, ..	5– 9–18
Dvr.	..	DUNN, E. ..	..	..	,, ..	16– 9–18
Gnr.	..	EARL, G. E.	..	..	,, ..	16– 9–18
Sergt.	..	McKENZIE, C. D.	..	..	,, ..	28– 9–18
Gnr.	..	FOSTER, S.	..	..	,, ..	29– 9–18
Dvr.	..	PREECE, W. E.	..	..	,, ..	28– 9–18
Bdr.	..	BULL, H. E.	..	..	Died of wounds ..	12–10–18
Dvr.	..	McADAM, J. H.	..	..	Killed in action ..	11–10–18
Dvr.	..	MURRAY, J.	..	..	,, ..	29– 9–18
Corpl.	..	COLLINS, T. E.	..	..	Wounded ..	12–10–18
Dvr.	..	PARKER, F. W.	..	..	Died of wounds ..	23–10–18
Dvr.	..	PERCIVAL, W. J.	..	..	Wounded ..	24–10–18
Dvr.	..	HASTE, W.	..	..	,, ..	24–10–18

Trench Mortar Batteries, 39th Div.

RANK.		NAME.			NATURE OF CASUALTY.	DATE.
Gnr.	..	HARDING, T.	..	..	Wounded	4– 8–17
Dvr.	..	SAMUELS, J.	..	..	,, ...	6– 8–17
Gnr.	..	WAKEFIELD, W.	..	..	Killed in action ..	15– 9–17
Gnr.	..	MULLINS, E. T.	..	..	Wounded	18– 9–17
Gnr.	..	SIDAWAY, J. A.	..	..	,, ..	16–10–17
Bdr.	..	SKIRROW, H.	..	..	,, ..	16–10–17
Gnr.	..	LAM, F. F.	..	..	,, ..	17–10–17
Gnr.	..	SUTHERS, A.	..	..	,, ..	23–10–17
Gnr.	..	PARISH, H.	..	..	,, ..	17–10–17

RANK.	NAME.	NATURE OF CASUALTY.	DATE.
Fitter ..	BOAST, J.	Wounded	25–10–17
Gnr. ..	SWARSBRICK, E.	,, ...	25–10–17
Dvr. ..	TURNER, F. F.	,, ...	22–10–17
Gnr. ..	LYNCH, P.	,, ...	17–10–17
Gnr. ..	GREEN, J.	,, ...	23–10–17
Gnr. ..	FLAHERTY, J.	Killed in action	17–11–17
Bdr. ..	ROACH, J. J.	Wounded	17–11–17
Dvr. ..	LEYSHAM, R.	,, ...	18–11–17
Dvr. ..	GORDAN, W. A. J. ..	,, ...	6–12–17
Bdr. ..	HILL, C.	Killed in action ..	6–12–17
Corpl. ..	WHEELER, A.	Wounded	11– 2–17
Dvr. ..	SUTTON, C. A.	Killed in action ..	10– 6–17
Dvr. ..	CONWAY, G. W.	Wounded	10– 6–17
Gnr. ..	DUNFORD, B.	,, ...	10– 6–17
Bdr. ..	EARL, E. G.	,, ...	10– 6–17
Dvr. ..	VEALE, A...	,, ...	10– 6–17
Dvr. ..	MICHAEL, A.	,, ...	10– 6–17
Dvr. ..	TURNER, F. F.	,, ...	16– 6–17
Gnr. ..	RISHWORTH, H.	,, ...	21– 6–17
Gnr. ..	BURGESS, R. C.	,, ...	16– 6–17
Dvr. ..	LEYSHAM, R.	,, ...	23– 6–17
Gnr. ..	TRUMP, J.	,, ...	14– 7–17
Gnr. ..	WESTERN, W.	,, ...	14– 7–17
Gnr. ..	McCANNA, W.	,, ...	23– 7–17
Dvr. ..	WRIGHT, W. C.	,, ...	1–11–16
Bdr. ..	LLEWELLYN, E.	,, ...	1–11–16
Dvr. ..	PATTERSON, W.	,, ...	13– 9–16
Gnr. ..	GRINSELL, E.	Killed in action ..	29– 9–18
Gnr. ..	RUSSELL, W.	,, ...	29– 9–16
Dvr. ..	BOWLEY, J. E.	,, ...	29– 9–16
Gnr. ..	GARDINER, A. G. ..	Wounded	10–10–16
Gnr. ..	STURNHAM, J. J. ..	,, ...	10–10–16
Gnr. ..	EVANS, F.	,, ...	19–11–16
Gnr. ..	TIBBITTS, B. J.	Killed in action ..	4– 2–17
Sergt. ..	PAYNE, H. E.	,, ...	25– 3–17
Bdr. ..	CHESSUM, E.	Wounded	15– 5–17
Sergt. ..	WALTON, C.	,, ...	15– 5–17
Gnr. ..	BLACKMORE, H. M. ..	,, ...	15– 5–17
Gnr. ..	BREHENEY, J.	,, ...	15– 5–17
Gnr. ..	BLACKBOURN, C. A. V. ..	Killed in action ..	19– 6–17
Dvr. ..	BEECHAM, A. J.	Wounded	19– 6–17
Dvr. ..	BUTLER, M.	,, ...	27– 6–17
Gnr. ..	PORTER, G. J.	,, ...	29–10–17
Gnr. ..	NUGENT, H. H.	,, ...	30– 6–17
Gnr. ..	CRADDOCK, W	,, ...	14– 7–16
Bdr. ..	JOHNSON, J.	,, ...	27– 3–18
Corpl. ..	LYWOOD, C. S.	,, ...	27– 3–18
Dvr. ..	BAKER, S.	,, ...	11– 5–18
Gnr. ..	JONES, R. P.	,, ...	3– 9–16
Gnr. ..	COKER, H. T.	,, ...	9– 9–16
Bdr. ..	ILES, G. R.	,, ...	27– 9–16
Gnr. ..	WILDS, A...	Killed in action ..	27– 9–16
Gnr. ..	BEAMISH, H. G.	Died of wounds ..	18–11–16
Corpl. ..	WATLER, T. G.	Wounded	10–11–16

RANK.		NAME.		NATURE OF CASUALTY.	DATE.
Bdr.	..	MIDDLETON, S. J.	..	Wounded	6–12–17
Gnr.	..	PARSONS, C. W. ..	..	,, ...	7– 1–17
Gnr.	..	WILLIAMS, F. ..	..	,, ...	25– 6–17
Dvr.	..	COLE, E. H. ..	..	,, ...	27– 6–17
Bdr.	..	NEWMAN, T. ..	..	,, ...	27– 6–17
Dvr.	..	THORN, J. G. ..	..	,, ...	26– 6–17
Dvr.	..	FEATHERSTONE, R.	..	,, ...	14– 7–17
Dvr.	..	TURNELL, W. ..	..	,, ...	26– 7–17
Dvr.	..	DEARDEN, W. ..	..	Killed in action ..	26– 7–17
Dvr.	..	SEARES, H. J. ..	..	Wounded ..	26– 7–17
Dvr.	..	MADDEN, W. ..	..	Killed in action ..	19– 9–17
Gnr.	..	ANDREWS, W. J.	..	,, ..	4– 6–16
Gnr.	..	LINGHAM, C. ..	..	Wounded ..	4– 6–16
Gnr.	..	LAWRENCE, G. ..	..	,, ..	4– 6–16
Gnr.	..	MITCHELL, W. ..	..	,, ..	4– 6–16
Gnr.	..	RIGOZZI, I. ..	..	,, ..	29– 6–16
Gnr.	..	COOPER, S. ..	..	,, ..	30– 6–16
Dvr.	..	HAMMOND, W. J.	..	,, ..	4– 4–18
Gnr.	..	McCALLUM, J. ..	..	,, ..	4– 4–18
Sergt.	..	WALTON, C., M.M.	..	,, ..	4– 4–18
Dvr.	..	COLE, C.	..	,, ..	15– 5–18
Gnr.	..	HALL, G.	..	Died of wounds ..	3– 9–16
Gnr.	..	MOLYNEUX, J. ..	..	Wounded ..	7– 9–16
Corpl.	..	SAWYER, G. F. ..	..	,, ..	10–10–16
Dvr.	..	WRIGHT, G. ..	..	,, ..	10–10–16
Gnr.	..	DUNSTER, J. J. ..	..	,, ..	16–10–16
Gnr.	..	PRICE, F. T. ..	..	Killed in action ..	6–12–17
Gnr.	..	GASKIN, G. E. ..	..	Wounded ..	21– 7–17
Gnr.	..	HIGGS, F. F. ..	..	,, ..	6– 8–17
Corpl.	..	SARGEANT, G. ..	..	,, ..	19– 9–17
Sergt.	..	MORTIMER, W. ..	..	,, ..	1–11–17
Gnr.	..	WHEATLEY, W. ..	..	,, ..	10– 2–17
Corpl.	..	UPTON, F. J. ..	..	,, ..	13– 2–17
Gnr.	..	BANNISTER, B. T.	..	Missing ..	28– 3–18
Gnr.	..	SWARSBRICK, E. ..	..	,, ..	28– 3–18
Gnr.	..	SKIRROW, H. ..	..	,, ..	28– 3–18
Gnr.	..	COUTANCHE, A. ..	..	,, ..	23– 3–18
Gnr.	..	WEILD, F. ..	..	,, ..	28– 3–18
Gnr.	..	GREEN, H. ..	..	,, ..	28– 3–18
Dvr.	..	McMASTER, W. ..	..	,, ..	28– 3–18
Corpl.	..	PIPER, E. P. ..	..	,, ..	28– 3–18
Corpl.	..	SPACKMAN, E. S.	..	,, ..	28– 3–18
Bdr.	..	STANLEY, G. R. ..	..	,, ..	28– 3–18
Gnr.	..	GARDINER, A. G.	..	,, ..	28– 3–18

HONOURS & AWARDS

39th Divisional Artillery.

MISCELLANEOUS AWARDS.

Brig.-Gen. G. Gillson	Order of Danilo, 3rd Class Promoted Brevet Colonel and Mentioned in Despatches.
Brig.-Gen. G. A. S. Cape ..	C.M.G.
Lt.-Col. E. W. S. Brooke ..	C.M.G.
T/Lt.-Col. J. G. B. Allardyce	Brevet Lt.-Col.
Major W. F. Nicholson ..	Cavalier of the Order of the Crown of Italy.

DISTINGUISHED SERVICE ORDER.

T/Lt.-Col. J. G. B. Allardyce.
A/Major G. T. Thomas.
Lt.-Col. C. A. Kilner.
Major G. E. M. Thorneycroft.
Major F. E. Spencer.
Lt.-Col. Lord A. E. Browne.

BAR TO MILITARY CROSS.

A/Major G. T. Thomas.
A/Major G. Heron.
A/Major W. Jones.

SECOND BAR TO MILITARY CROSS.

A/Major G. Heron.

MILITARY CROSS.

T/Capt. O. C. K. Corrie.
2/Lieut. J. E. Sierra.
A/Major G. C. Kemp.
A/Major J. J. J. Bell.
Capt. G. I. Thomas.
T/Capt. G. Heron.
A/Major W. Strachan.
A/Capt. E. C. L. Kilkelly.
2/Lieut. S. R. Barham.
2/Lieut. H. F. Barnes.
A/Major W. B. Telling.
2/Lieut. R. C. Rodger.
2/Lieut. F. V. Wallington.
Capt. H. W. Wiebkin.
B.S.M. Hines, H. W.
2/Lieut. P. C. Richards.
2/Lieut. C. A. Wilson.
Lieut. J. B. Tremlett.
2/Lieut. D. S. Doig.
2/Lieut. R. E. Huston.
2/Lieut. C. B. H. Delamain.
2/Lieut. J. A. Casserley.
2/Lieut. J. E. Warner.
Lieut. C. W. Longley.
2/Lieut. F. Wilde.
2/Lieut. G. D. Shaw.
Lieut. O. N. Mash.
2/Lieut. N. Walker.
Lieut. R. A. Young.
A/Capt. J. Lamb.
A/Major G. L. K. Wiseley.
A/Major P. Wright.
T/Capt. H. F. Burke.
2/Lieut. D. E. Kemp.
A/Capt. J. A. W. Griffiths.
A/Major K. O. Siedle.
2/Lieut. T. J. Wilford.
2/Lieut. D. McCunn.
2/Lieut. W. F. Rattle.
2/Lieut. H. W. H. Beaumont.
2/Lieut. H. L. Jupp.
A/Capt. V. S. Bland.
A/Capt. T. Mulligan.
2/Lieut. E. L. Vale.
2/Lieut. F. R. Rice.
2/Lieut. F. S. Tocher.

OFFICERS MENTIONED IN DESPATCHES.

A/Major K. O. SIEDLE.
Major F. G. SPENCER.
2/Lieut. F. D. O'DELL.
Major C. C. PHILLIPS.
T/Capt. H. D. TYLER.
Major W. S. NICHOLSON.
2/Lieut. R. W. SPOONER.
Lieut. E. J. L. BENNETT.
2/Lieut. F. STRAKER.
2/Lieut. A. S BARNES.
Lieut. G. S. GOODALL.
2/Lieut. S. R. BARHAM.
Lt.-Col. C. H. KILNER.
Major Hon. B. J. RUSSELL.
Capt. M. B. HEATH.
2/Lieut. S. C. LAMB.
2/Lieut. G. D. SHAW.
2/Lieut. G. A. WILSON.
Lieut. V. HILL.
Capt. H. C. SCHOLEFIELD.

Capt. J. E. SHEFFIELD.
Major W. B. TELLING.
Capt. A. E. DELGADS, R.A.M.C.
Major F. E. SPENCER.
Major W. B. TELLING.
A/Major W. STRACHAN.
A/Major G. C. KEMP.
A/Capt. J. B. ROBERTON.
A/Capt. V. HILL.
Lieut. W. M. DOBSON.
2/Lieut. J. E. H. P. THOMPSON.
2/Lieut. E. V. JOHNSON.
A/Capt. J. A. W. GRIFFITH.
A/Major W. JONES.
A/Capt. E. F. CROWDY.
A/Capt. J. E. SHEFFIELD.
Lieut. W. J. MOSS.
A/Capt. V. HILL.
Lieut. O. C. ROSSITER.

DISTINGUISHED CONDUCT MEDAL.

RANK.	NAME.	UNIT.
Corpl.	HALLOWS	174th Brigade, R.F.A.
B.S.M.	WRIGHT	186th ,,
Sergt.	TROTH	174th ,,
Bdr.	JONES	186th ,,
Corpl.	WALKER	174th ,,
B.S.M.	BRYANT	174th ,,
B.S.M.	LOW	186th ,,
Sergt.	ABRAHAM	174th ,,
B.Q.M.S.	FROUD	186th ,,
B.S.M.	BARLOW	174th ,,
B.S.M.	BARNES	186th ,,
Driver	HAMES	174th ,,
Sergt.	HIRD	186th ,,
A/Sergt.	HEY, R.E.	H.Q. 186th Brigade, R.F.A. (attached)
B.S.M.	KELLY	186th Brigade, R.F.A.

MILITARY MEDAL.

Sergt	KNIBBS	Trench Mortars.
Corpl.	CROOKS	,,
Corpl.	RICHARDS	,,
Gnr.	ILES	,,
Gnr.	CROXEN	,,
Bdr.	CUTTS	,,
Bdr.	STEWART	174th Brigade, R.F.A.
Gnr.	PRAGNELL	174th ,,

MILITARY MEDAL.

RANK.	NAME.	UNIT.
A/Bdr.	FANNING	174th Brigade, R.F.A.
Bdr.	WOOD	184th ,,
Bdr.	CHAPMAN	186th ,,
Gnr.	CLAYDON	186th ,,
Gnr.	WILLIAMS, W.	186th ,,
Gnr.	PULLEN	186th ,,
Gnr.	MATHEWS	186th ,,
Bdr.	SEAL	186th ,,
Sergt.	WALTON	Trench Mortars.
Sergt.	JELLYMAN	186th Brigade, R.F.A.
Bdr.	ROONEY	186th ,,
Bdr.	SNOW	174th ,,
Sergt.	MURRAY	174th ,,
Bdr.	FLETCHER	174th ,,
Gnr.	CONNOLLEY	174th ,,
Sergt.	KING	186th ,,
Gnr.	MITCHELL	186th ,,
Corpl.	HOLDEN	D.A.C.
Dvr...	ARNETT	,,
Sergt.	SKIPPER	,,
Bdr.	CARSTAIRS	174th Brigade, R.F.A.
Bdr.	JEEVES	174th ,,
Fitter	LEVITAS	
Sergt.	THOMAS	186th Brigade, R.F.A.
Sergt.	ABRAHAM	174th ,,
Bdr.	LUHMAN	174th ,,
Sergt.	BAILEY	186th ,,
Corpl.	PENROSE	174th ,,
Sergt.	HEY	R.E., att. H.Q. 186th Bde.
A/Sergt.	HALLS	R.E., att. H.Q. 174th Bde.
Sergt.	MAILLARDET	174th Brigade, R.F.A.
Sergt.	WINTERS	174th ,,
Sergt.	GALVIN	174th ,,
Gnr.	KINLEY	186th ,,
Bdr.	CATLEY	174th ,,
Sergt.	SCRIVENS	186th ,,
Sergt.	STAMFORD	D.A.C.
Dvr...	SPENCER	174th Brigade, R.F.A.
Dvr...	SWEETMAN	174th ,,
Bdr.	MACK	174th ,,
Gnr.	STEIN	174th ,,
Bdr.	PATMORE	174th ,,
A/Bdr.	CAREY	186th ,,
Gnr.	HARRAWAY	186th ,,
Corpl.	THRUSSELL	D.A.C.
Dvr...	HOARE	,,
Dvr...	RAWLINGS	,,
Sergt.	HUBBLE	Trench Mortars
Sergt.	ADAMS	186th Brigade, R.F.A.
Sergt.	MONTEITH	186th ,,
Sergt.	GIBSON	186th ,,
Corpl.	WILDE	D.A.C.

MILITARY MEDAL.

RANK.	NAME.	UNIT.
Corpl. ..	Cook	D.A.C.
Gnr. ..	Bryan	174th Brigade, R.F.A.
Corpl. ..	Benning..	174th ,,
Fitter ..	White	174th ,,
Gnr. ..	Manley	174th ,,
Bdr. ..	Drew	186th ,,
Gnr. ..	Long	186th ,,
Gnr. ..	McNamara	174th ,,
L/Bdr. ..	King	186th ,,
Dvr... ..	Pugh	186th ,,
Sergt. ..	Harris	186th ,,
Dvr... ..	Stubbs	186th ,,
Dvr... ..	Thompson	186th ,,
L/Corpl. ..	Brighton	R.E., att. H.Q. D.A.
Spr. ..	Woodfield	,,
Spr. ..	Ward	,,
Corpl. ..	Jordon	,,
Dvr... ..	Stallwood	174th Brigade. R.F.A.
Bdr. ..	Flynn	174th ,,
Sergt. ..	Hird	186th ,,
Sergt. ..	Simpson	174th ,,
Dvr... ..	Beckson..	174th ,,
Sergt. ..	Buckland	186th ,,
Gnr. ..	Stephenson	186th ,,
Bdr. ..	Battye	174th ,,
Sergt. ..	Bishop	174th ,,
Gnr. ..	Ball	174th ,,
L/Bdr. ..	Smith	186th ,,
Dvr... ..	East	186th ,,
Sergt. ..	McKenzie	D.A.C.
Gnr. ..	Beecroft	174th Brigade, R.F.A.
Sergt. ..	Patterson	174th ,,
Farr/Sergt. ..	Anderson	174th ,,
Bdr. ..	Ealham	174th ,,
Gnr. ..	Evan	174th ,,
Corp . ..	Ashcroft	R.E., att. H.Q. 186th Bde.
Bdr. ..	Hughes	186th Brigade, R.F.A.
Dvr... ..	Watson	174th ,,
Bdr. ..	Bailey	174th ,,
Gnr. ..	Osborne..	174th ,,
Gnr. ..	Price	174th ,,
Gnr. ..	Walker	186th ,,
Sergt. ..	Bailey	186th ,,
L/Bdr. ..	Cockell	186th ,,
Gnr. ..	Chenery	186th ,,
Bdr. ..	Gantry	186th ,,
Corpl. ..	Andrews	186th ,,
Gnr. ..	Melville	186th ,,

BAR TO MILITARY MEDAL.

RANK.	NAME.	UNIT.
A/Bdr. ..	GENTRY	174th Brigade, R.F.A.
Sergt. ..	HARRIS	186th ,,
Corpl. ..	JEEVES	174th ,,
Gnr. ..	BUTCHER	174th ,,
Corpl. ..	MITCHELL	186th ,,

MERITORIOUS SERVICE MEDAL.

B.S.M. ..	COTTON	174th Brigade, R.F.A.
Sergt. ..	MCKENZIE	D.A.C.
Dvr... ..	MACK	174th Brigade, R.F.A.
Sergt. ..	ROBERTSON	Trench Mortars.
B.S.M. ..	HART	174th ,,
Sergt. ..	ROBINSON	186th ,,
Ftr/S/Sergt.	BARBER	186th ,,
Sergt. ..	BELL	186th ,,
Sergt. ..	STOCKWELL	174th ,,
Ftr/Corpl. ..	HUMPHRIES	174th ,,
Gnr. ..	HOOPER	D.A.C.

MENTIONS IN DESPATCHES (O.R.s).

A/Bdr. ..	SPINNER	184th Brigade, R.F.A.
Corpl. ..	O'DRISCOLL	179th ,,
Bdr. ..	HIRD	184th ,,
Corpl. ..	DOUGHTY	D.A.C.
B.S.M. ..	HART	174th Brigade, R.F.A.
Corpl. ..	BRYAN	174th ,,
Sergt. ..	HIRD	186th ,,
Bdr. ..	TYNSK	186th ,,
Sergt. ..	ABRAHAM	174th ,,
A/B.S.M. ..	MCKENZIE	D.A.C.
Sergt. ..	JAMES	D.A.C.
Corpl. ..	HALLS	174th Brigade, R.F.A.
S.M. (W.O.1)	WESTON	H.Q. Divnl. Artillery.
Sergt. ..	HEY, W. H.	B/186th Brigade, R.F.A.
Sergt. ..	JOHNSON	D.A.C.

$$
\begin{array}{r}
54 \\
34 \\
\hline
1620 \\
216 \\
\hline
1836 \\
42 \\
\hline
1878 \\
28 \\
\hline
1906 \\
\end{array}
$$

Printed in the United Kingdom
by Lightning Source UK Ltd.
113491UKS00001B/370

9 781845 740825